THEOLOGY
for Parents and Teachers
by Father Melvin L. Farrell, S.S.

THEOLOGY FOR PARENTS AND TEACHERS is the result of 24 articles which appeared as a weekly feature of the 1971-72 *Better Teaching*, the teacher's edition of HI-TIME, the weekly high school religion text. Father Melvin L. Farrell, S.S., S.T.D., wrote the articles in order to help teachers and parents understand current theological teaching and to give them a solid basis for presenting Catholic doctrine. The 24 easy-to-read, easy-to-understand articles are now gathered under one cover, THEOLOGY FOR PARENTS AND TEACHERS.

Nihil Obstat
Monsignor
John Francis Murphy, S.T.D.

Censor Librorum
Imprimatur
† William E. Cousins
Archbishop of Milwaukee
July 16, 1971

PHOTOS:

11 36 49 51 55 62 71 84
RICHARD F. BAUER
66 81 88 JOHN W. AHLHAUSER
26 GEORGE R. CASSIDY
33 JOHN BURR CAVAN
14 WILLIAM DREHFAL
23 FATHER KEITH EGAN. O. CAR
76 JACK HAMILTON
93 RONALD M. OVERDAHL
GRAPHICS: JEFFERY PARNAU

HI-TIME Publishers, Inc.
Box 7337
Milwaukee, Wisconsin 53213

Contents

Introduction

BY FATHER JOHN R. McCALL, S.J., Ph.D.

What a pleasure it is to be able to write a few words of introduction to this book by Father Melvin Farrell. As I understand it, an introduction should be brief enough not to intrude on the book, but long enough to introduce the author and make you want to read his book.

I have known Father Farrell for many years. And his book is so good that I have read and reread it. I can tell you, therefore, that he moves with a great light touch, but with a deep scholarship, from the question "What Happened to the Baltimore Catechism?" to his chapter on "Is Confession Old-Fashioned?" Through it all you meet a man who is not only a profound theologian and an experienced teacher, but a person who is gifted with the ability to write in such a way that even the most profound teachings are interesting and alive as they come from his pen.

At this time Father Farrell is rector of Saint Patrick Seminary in the Archdiocese of San Francisco, but he has great experience in teaching at all levels. He has his doctorate from the Catholic University of America. As some of you may know, his writing for HI-TIME and for *Focus on* HOPE has been acclaimed throughout the United States, Canada and Australia. People who have had an opportunity to read Father Farrell's writings in the past praise him for his ability to simplify the complicated, without oversimplifying it. With the balance of a good theologian, he always looks to the future, but never without looking to the past. He is always very much present to what is going on in the world around him. His own teaching has helped him to be an excellent guide to those who need help in learning how to communicate the word of God through religious education.

Father Farrell's book is both theoretical and practical, profound and yet easy to understand. It will be of inestimable help in preparing teachers to meet young students in the field of religious search. All through these excellent chapters, I have been amazed at how alive Father Farrell is able to make theology. For instance, he says:

> To understand the changing vocabulary of grace today, we must ask ourselves what the traditional terms really meant, and why they are no longer considered to be adequate.
>
> The word "grace" is found in the Bible; the term "sanctifying grace" is not. We have been so conditioned by the latter term that we equate it with the biblical word "grace." For example, in the revised standard version of the Bible, when we read " . . . by grace you have been saved . . . " (Ephesians 2:8), we assume that Saint Paul means sanctifying grace. In fact, however, Paul knew nothing of our terminology. He uses "grace" pretty much as a synonym for "gift." In this passage, as in his other writings, Paul is not hinting obliquely at a later theology of grace. Instead, he is emphasizing the fact that salvation comes to us as a free, unmerited gift from God. This is quite a different matter.

pages 47-48

These words of Father Mel Farrell will help you and me to develop a better understanding of the meaning of our salvation as we come to appreciate what Christ has freely given us. Then we shall come to know and love Christ more.

At no time does Father try to impose certainty where there is none, but he always opens up new doors so that we can search with great hope. I cannot recommend this book too highly, and I am grateful to be able to write these words of introduction.

1

What Is Religious Education Today?

When I was in high school, religion classes were much like other courses. A certain amount of material had to be learned. The course was laid out in the black-and-white certitudes, the precise questions and the precise answers, of a catechism. The atmosphere was serious. No goofing off was tolerated. Competition for gold stars and fear of flunking motivated us. At least, we seemed to learn "religion."

Or did we? What is religion? In theory, we all know the answer to this question. Religion has to do with man's relationship with God. But let's be practical. What does religion mean in practice for the average churchgoer? Here is the analysis of Father Josef Jungmann, S.J., one of the Church's most respected theologians for the past 30 years. Father Jungmann finds that "Catholicism has become a traditional confession" in which customs and practices are sustained by community pressures. He talks about a Catholicism whose

"religious capital consists for the most part in a sum of obligations — an uninspiring series of 'musts' and 'don'ts' " which must be followed by a person if he is to save his soul (*The Good News, Yesterday and Today*. New York, W. H. Sadlier, 1962, page 3).

It is noteworthy that Father Jungmann wrote these words in 1936, long before Vatican II inspired a major overhaul in religious education. The words ring just as true today.

Recently, a 15-year-old boy, brilliant for his age but in deep psychic trouble, blurted out that he wanted to use his life making the world a better place. But religion, as he saw it, gave him no vision and no challenge. He understood religion exactly as Father Jungmann described it. The young man spoke for many others.

What, then, is religion? More to the point, what is Christianity? Whatever definitions we learned as children, Catholics have always held that Christianity is exactly what Christ and the apostolic Church meant it to be. With good reason, then, theologians and religious educators today have probed the original content of our inherited faith. With the help of modern scholarship and the encouragement of Vatican II, the Christian message has been carefully unearthed from its historical foundations and traced to the present.

Three insights of crucial importance have come to light.

1. The original Christian message, the gospel, hinges totally on this belief: Jesus of Nazareth was raised up from death by God so that, as Christ the Lord, He can now impart life without end to all men.

2. This simple but all-inclusive belief organically unfolded throughout history into the elaborate system of faith and practice familiar to us as Catholics today.

3. Many historical developments in Christianity arose to meet the needs of a given cultural situation. Unfortunately, when these temporary accommodations became obsolete, they were sometimes retained and began to obscure the deeper meaning of the gospel.

Applying these insights to the current scene in religious education, we can begin to understand what is happening and why.

In the first place, most adult Catholics today lack a right understanding of the gospel, the core message of Christian faith. They have been taught the fundamental dogmas of the Church, as well as its operational structures. They know the commandments, and the meaning of sin. They know the seven sacraments. But they have little familiarity with the gospel message itself, which is supposedly the life's blood of their religion.

The cause underlying this distressing fact is to be found in history. The stage was set for this situation at the time of the Protestant revolt. The Council of Trent, which dealt with the Protestant crisis, placed the Catholic Church in a strongly defensive posture. What was necessary at the time was to justify the Catholic Church and to argue down the claims of the Protestant reformers. In effect, religious education from that time up to Vatican II aimed at the very same goals. With the Church under siege from rival religious bodies, the gospel message became secondary to an exact understanding of the Roman Catholic Church.

Vatican II put an official close to this era of warfare, and invited Protestants to join us in a common search to recapture the authentic spirit of the gospel. But Vatican II did more. Applying established conclusions of contemporary theological studies, Vatican II with its 16 documents heralded a new and exciting age for theology and, therefore, for religious education.

The *Pastoral Constitution on the Church in the Modern World* calls for a revised statement of the gospel message in keeping with the contemporary mind and the insights of modern theology. The Council Fathers point out that the world today is experiencing a great cultural revolution, affecting man's " . . . decisions and desires, both individual and collective, and . . . his manner of thinking and acting with respect to things and to people" (article 4). At the same time, " . . . recent studies and findings of science, history, and philosophy raise new questions which affect life and demand new theologi-

The perennial freshness of the original gospel message is being reaffirmed

cal investigations" (article 62). As a result, religious education must be updated. "Indeed, this accommodated preaching of the revealed Word ought to remain the law of all evangelization" (article 44).

In religious education today, newness of approach is twofold. First, the message is being dramatically revised and updated. The outmoded doctrinal baggage of post-Reformation catechisms is being discarded. The perennial freshness of the original gospel message is being reaf-

firmed. This new approach to the content of religious education touches every facet of religion as we were taught it a generation ago. The meaning of the Church, sacraments, and morality is coming through in ways more relevant and attractive to people today. More important, the new approach echoes authentic Christian understanding more accurately than was formerly the case.

Second, the manner in which religion is taught today is also new. The change is partly due to the electronic age in which our children have grown up, and the altered way in which they learn. But religious education is doing more than borrowing updated teaching techniques from secular education. The most revolutionary doctrinal insight of modern theology is that Christianity primarily has to do with persons, rather than with doctrines, and with what is happening, rather than with what has happened. The person of Jesus Christ, alive and active in history today, is the heart of the message. Religious education, therefore, is not so much a matter of studying definitions as it is a matter of discovering Christ in one's personal experience. This realization calls for a new understanding of what should go on in the religion class.

Our purpose in this first chapter has been to sketch, in large black-and-white strokes, the historical setting for the current revolution in teaching religion. The strokes are accurate, but they must be filled in. This we will do in succeeding chapters.

2

What Happened to the Baltimore Catechism?

Have you ever put aside a perfectly good piece of clothing for a year or two, only to react with disappointment when you take it out? Somehow it has grown old, or out of style, or does not fit properly. Things human are like that. The Baltimore catechism, despite its venerable past, is something human. It has grown old, out of style, and does not fit today's needs properly.

In the previous chapter, we saw that the changes in religious education today stem from two causes, both affirmed in the documents of the Second Vatican Council. First, theology in recent years has introduced significant changes both in the expression of our traditional belief as Catholics and in its understanding. A more accurate grasp of the original gospel message lies at the heart of these shifts in theological perspective. Second, cultural change, which characterizes modern life on

a global scale, has altered man's view of himself and of his world, his world view.

This is to say that on two counts the Baltimore catechism suffers from obsolescence. Its theology is dated and out of harmony with important developments since Vatican II. Also, its cultural frame of reference, the world view it assumes throughout, belongs to a generation of the past.

Before we examine this obsolescence in more detail, it would be helpful to review a few key historical facts about the Baltimore catechism. It was first written in the closing days of the Third Plenary Council of Baltimore of 1884. The first draft was hurriedly done by Monsignor Januarius De Concilio, a pastor from Jersey City serving the council as an advising theologian. Some refinement followed, but the first edition was published a few months after the council was over.

Public reaction to the new religion text was not enthusiastic. In fact, criticism was so loud and persistent that in 1896 the American bishops appointed a committee to revise the work. The committee's project dragged on for several years. With the death of the committee chairman in 1903, the work came to a halt. Not until 1935 was the task undertaken again. This time, however, the assignment was carried out. The revised Baltimore catechism appeared in 1941, dominating the religious education scene in America until roughly the dawn of Vatican II.

One might ask why the original Baltimore catechism was allowed to remain unchanged for so long in time, since it was widely conceded from the start that the work was deficient. There are several reasons, but by far the most important cause was what is known as the Modernist crisis. This movement stemmed from Church-state struggles in France and in Italy, from biblical and historical research in Germany, and from the theory of biological evolution. Such developments urged doctrinal reform and seemed to undermine traditional understandings of the faith. Around the turn of the century, in reaction to bad experiences, the Church entered a period of retrenchment and defensiveness toward modern science. The problem was that certain theories, including evolution, seemed to undermine traditional understandings of the faith.

Not certain how to handle threats posed by secular science, the Church concentrated on shoring up the underpinnings of traditional formulations of the faith. In effect, for the first half of the present century, theology was locked in a deep freeze. There was enormous opposition to changes of any kind. As a result, religious education tended to give people a Rock-of-Gibraltar concept of their faith. This is one reason that Catholic adults today find it so difficult to cope with the changes thrust upon them since Vatican II.

Vatican II marked the bursting of the defensive dike erected by the Church at the beginning of the century. The initial change of policy toward modern science came in 1943, with Pius XII's encyclical, *Divino Afflante Spiritu*. The modern movement in theology dates from this time, and slowly gained momentum until its decisive impact on the proceedings of the Council Fathers of Vatican II.

Because the revised Baltimore catechism came out in 1941, it was untouched by the modern theological renewal. Loyal to the mood of anti-Modernism, it presents the faith exactly as the original Baltimore catechism did. The revised version is more coherent and clear, but its substance is identical with that of its predecessor. Moreover, the cultural world view of the 1884 catechism remains unchanged in the 1941 edition — so reluctant was the revision committee to allow any change in the traditional statement of faith.

Now let us ask the question: Precisely how is the Baltimore catechism obsolete in its theology and in its cultural world view?

The theology underlying the Baltimore catechism represents a post-Reformation idea of the faith. Its controlling concern is doctrinal exactness with an anti-Protestant thrust. Like all post-Reformation catechisms, it emphasizes what Protestants deny, and plays down what Protestants uphold. For example, Protestants extol the Bible as a rule of faith and tend to ignore tradition. The Baltimore catechism, therefore, pretty much ignores the Bible and relies heavily on sacred tradition. Protestants view the Church mainly as a spiritual, invisible reality composed of those who believe in Christ. The Baltimore catechism presents the Church almost entirely in terms of its visible organization, complete with its hierarchy of pope, bishops, priests and laity. Similar examples abound.

The root fault here is that controversies are allowed to obscure a true and balanced understanding of what the gospel is saying and of what it means to a right grasp of divine revelation, the Church, the sacraments. In succeeding chapters, we will take up these elements of our faith in detail. For now, suffice it to say that Vatican II and post-conciliar theology approach these concepts quite differently than does the Baltimore catechism.

The world view of 1884 was in sharp contrast with that of today. Communications, transportation, and technology were in their infancy in 1884. Now that the age of telstar, rock records, and space travel are upon us, the younger generation, in particular, view life with a different shade of cultural sunglasses than their ancestors did. They look upon the physical universe, history, man, and religion itself from a very different perspective.

Christ said we should not put new wine into old wineskins. This holds for the updated theology of Vatican II. The world view of the Baltimore catechism is as outmoded as the Stanley steamer. It made sense 50 years ago, even 20 years ago. But it makes less and less sense as the contemporary, cultural revolution goes on.

For example, the Baltimore catechism conveys its entire message in terms of *obligations*. We are told what we *must* believe (Creed), what we *must* do (commandments), and what means we *must* use (sacraments), in order to be saved. Today it is well known that young people are on a freedom kick. The cultural context makes them this way. To present Christianity as a series of obligations is to make the message, of its very nature, threatening. It turns the good news of the gospel into bad news!

What happened to the Baltimore catechism? Like other honored relics, it is being placed on the shelf of past history. It did the American Catholic people an immense service in its day. But its day is definitely over.

3

Divine Revelation: What Is It?

Divine revelation is a term which most adult Catholics recall, perhaps with some fuzziness, from their childhood religion classes. It is one of those abstract terms with which religion classes used to abound. But the term is a crucial one. It refers to whatever God communicates to man in a supernatural way.

To teach religion is, quite simply, to serve as a channel between divine revelation and students. Put that baldly, the task seems to be simple. Indeed, not long ago many a person's concept of teaching religion was simple. It was assumed that divine revelation amounts to a certain list of truths. These truths are set forth by the official teaching office of the Church, drawing upon the two sources of divine revelation: the Bible and sacred tradition. The catechism is a summary of these truths, digested and simplified for the young. To teach religion, then, was to teach the contents of the catechism.

The linch-pin in this former theory of religious education is the starting assumption: namely, that divine revelation is contained in propositional statements. Pull out this linch-pin and the whole theory falls apart. This is precisely what has happened.

The propositional theory of divine revelation was laid to rest by Vatican II. A key sentence in the *Dogmatic Constitution on Divine Revelation* reads:

> . . . Jesus perfected revelation by fulfilling it through the whole work of making Himself present and manifesting Himself: through His words and deeds, His signs and wonders, but especially through His death and glorious resurrection from the dead and final sending of the Spirit of truth.
>
> (article 4)

Note that divine revelation here is not limited to verbal statements. It includes Jesus' deeds, as well as His words. And the climax of revelation is declared to be the *events* of Good

Friday, of Easter, and of Pentecost.

This expansion of the former idea of revelation, which takes in the entire person of Jesus Christ and what is accomplished through Him, is tremendously important. The Fathers of Vatican II knew fully well the popular notion that revelation is essentially found in dogmatic pronouncements of the Church. In fact, in an earlier draft of the document they defined revelation in this way. But something happened to make them change their minds. Advising

> **God is the God not of the dead past, but of the living present**

theologians showed that the verbal theory of revelation, despite its acceptance for many years, did not accord with an earlier, more authentic understanding. This discovery prompted the Council Fathers to twice revise their original draft on revelation. The final document reflects a dramatically new approach to the subject.

The intervention of theologians in this case, typical of their influence throughout the Second Vatican Council, was based upon painstaking and solid research. Here we cannot touch on all the evidence supporting their conclusions. We will limit our attention to two insights having great practical bearing on religion teaching.

First, divine revelation is rooted primarily in historical events, and only secondarily in verbal statements about these events. The exodus event, Israel's journey from Egypt to the promised land, is a good example. What meant most for the Israelites was not what Moses said as God's spokesman, but what God did for them. He freed them from slavery. He fed them in the desert and protected them from enemy attack. He brought them safely into a land of their very own. These actions, more than any words, were divine revelation for the Jewish people. We, too, know that "actions speak louder than words."

Jesus Christ is the sum and substance of divine revelation. The Word Incarnate is divine revelation in His entire person. He not only teaches truth, He is the Truth (John 14:6). His earthly life is an historical event which makes God known in a surpassing way: ". . . Whoever has seen me has seen the Father" (John 14:9). In His acts of kindness and compassion, in His emotions and life-style, Jesus revealed the Father. Most of all in His act of dying and rising, Jesus made God known to us, as the Council Fathers declare.

What this means is that divine revelation is something more complex than verbal statements. The events which are verbally recorded in the Bible are an integral part of divine revelation. These events are not contained, nor are they exhaustively explained, in verbal statements. The Bible and the dogmas of the Church do not constitute divine revelation; they unerringly point to it. The reality must be sought beyond the words, however.

Second, divine revelation is something which continues to happen in the present as well as something which happened in the past. Jesus Christ, who is divine revelation, belongs as much to the present as to the past. He is risen and alive in power today. He is actively at work in the Church and in the world today. He, therefore, continues to reveal the Father, and His salvation plan for mankind, today.

Historical revelation, what has taken place in the past, is the basis for our faith, but it is not the focal point of our faith. God is the God not of the dead past, but of the living present. The Bible and sacred tradition are the means by which we detect Christ in our midst today. They serve as a mirror by which we can discover Christ's reflection in the present. Access to firsthand knowledge of Jesus' earthly activities came to a close with the death of the last apostle. In this sense revelation, in its foundational form, came to a close. But the person of Jesus, the undying source of divine revelation, lives on. And as the Church continues to experience Christ anew, divine revelation continues to happen.

To teach religion, then, is indeed to unfold the meaning of divine revelation to students. But this does not mean exclusively nor even primarily to teach propositional truths. Far more important, it means to guide students into an experience of the ongoing event of Jesus Christ. It means to help students to discern the presence and action of Christ in their own lives, in their personal experience. For Christ is really there, inviting their recognition and response. The teacher's task is no more nor less than to help students discover Christ for themselves.

Christ, then, cannot be equated with the words written in the Bible, nor with the dogmatic teachings of the Church. He is the One who pervades the cosmos, since all things have been made through Him. He dominates the history of the human race from beginning to end, since He is its Lord. He lies at the core of each man's search for truth and life, since He is the Way, the Truth and the Life. He is to be discovered in the world as well as in the Church, for He is the world's salvation.

This realization renders obsolete the catechism approach. Christ today is not to be found in formularies of the past, no matter how sacred. Statements of the past are indispensable tools, but our central task is to make students aware of Christ's present relationship to the present world. We must open their eyes, and unstop their ears, so that they can discover Him at the center of their own vital experience. This makes religion teaching a whole new ball game.

4

Is This Really the Same Church?

Beneath much of the confusion troubling the Church today are conflicting notions of what the Church is. Why do some people applaud the new style of celebrating Mass, while others are upset? Why are some complaining that the Church is becoming too "Protestant," while others say Rome is foot-dragging in the ecumenical movement? A sermon on social problems draws such opposite reactions as: religion and politics don't mix; and, it's about time the Church started speaking out on political issues. Why is this? Because people have competing ideas about the Church itself.

Within the past 25 years, in popular Catholic understanding it is possible to distinguish three different models of the Church at work. By carefully studying them, we find an excellent base for coming to grips with much of the confusion besetting the average man in the pew.

The first model of the Church can be described as the ghetto concept. Rooted in the Baltimore cat-echism and similar texts, this image of the Church grew out of the turmoil following the Protestant Reformation in the sixteenth century. At the time, the dominating concern of theologians was to emphasize the Catholic Church as an institution clearly distinguishable from other Christian bodies. The Catholic Church was defined in terms of its visible structures. It was portrayed as an organization whole and complete in itself, surrounded by an indifferent or hostile world. The distinctive structures by which this model can be recognized are the papacy, the hierarchy, its uniform liturgy and laws, and its clearly defined body of religious truths.

The ghetto image of the Church is not wrong; it is incomplete. What it lacks is a balanced understanding of the Church's responsibility toward the world. The dynamic outward thrust of the apostolic Church, which remained strong for centuries, began to die down rather noticeably after the Reformation. It could not have been otherwise. When a man's house is on fire, he is in no position to host the neighbors. When the Protestant break occurred, the Church had to bend all its energies to shore up crumbling foundations.

Inevitably, however, the Catholic Church yielded more and more to isolationism. It became a ghetto, closed in on itself. The "bark of Peter" was captained single-handedly by the pope. The bishops were viewed as the officers of the ship and priests and religious as the crew. Where did the laity fit into the picture? Here is the rub. The laity were viewed as paying passengers. They had no active role in the Church. As one bishop put it at the Second Vatican Council, the laity were expected only to pay, pray, and obey.

Catholics raised on the ghetto idea of the Church tend to regard themselves as an elite group to whom salvation belongs as an exclusive privilege. They are members of the Church in order to be saved. They do not deny the Church's obligation to offer salvation to others; indeed, they support missionary programs. Yet to their way of thinking, missionary work is something the Church does as a sideline. Its first concern is to tend to its own flock and shield them from the world's contagion.

The modern theological revival has gradually given rise to a new dimension in the Church's self-understanding. We can call this second model the missionary image of the Church. Around the mid-twentieth century, the Church started to shed the defensiveness which had characterized it ever since the Reformation. It found itself relating more easily, often on a friendly basis, with Protestant Churches. More important, studies in theology made the Catholic Church keenly aware of a forgotten responsibility toward the world at large.

The Church was founded by Christ to continue His work. His work is saving all men. It is wrong, therefore, for the Church to be almost totally absorbed in internal concerns. It must reach out to the world.

> **The leaven model of the Church has an outward dynamism**

This realization brought about a fresh burst of missionary interest in the Church, just prior to the Second Vatican Council.

Since the Second Vatican Council, however, a third phase of development in the Church's self-understanding has taken hold. It can be called a leaven image of the Church. The missionary model of the Church did not go far enough because it remained closely wedded to the ghetto image. As missionary image, the Church continued to be viewed essentially as a closed society, admitting only that it should take far more initiative in winning converts. The basic thrust of the Church remained inward, directed to itself. The leaven model of the Church has an outward dynamism. Today the Church is increasingly understood as the *servant of mankind*.

Building upon the Vatican II documents on the Church, theologians, in recent years, have uncovered, as never before, the original understanding of what the Church is supposed to be. The first centuries of the Church were dominated by the leaven image, found in Matthew 13:33. The Church saw itself as a Spirit-filled organization impregnating mankind with the saving power of Christ. It viewed its purpose in terms of three functions, each directed to the world at large.

First, the Church must proclaim the gospel, the good news that God is remaking mankind through His Son Jesus, offering men the transforming gift of Christ's Spirit freely bestowed through faith and Baptism.

The second task is to embody the gospel in a tangible way, namely, through fellowship, or a community of believers mutually committed to one another: "This is how all will know you for my disciples: your love for one another" (John 13:35). This fellowship is vivified through liturgical prayer, especially the Eucharist.

Finally, the task of the Church is to witness Christ to the world through service. As portrayed in the gospels, Jesus is eminently a man for others. He insists that He comes to serve, not to be served. His heart goes out to the poor, the needy, and the suffering members of the human race. It is through Jesus' ministry of compassion and healing that He is identified as Saviour of men. A like ministry should identify the Church. It is "the body of Christ" — the visible manifestation of Christ Himself among mankind. The Church, then, must serve the world's needy, and thus bear witness to the reality of Christ's saving love and power.

Gospel, fellowship, service: these are the three essential elements of the Church as Christ established it, and as it was understood from the beginning. Christ gave His Church certain organizational structures to unify it, to stabilize it, and to preserve it until the end of time. Yet all of these structures are subordinate to the Church's three basic functions in relation to mankind as a whole.

Is this really the same Church? Definitely yes. But it is a Church recovering from a long historical siege of defensiveness and inwardness. It is a Church renewing its youth by recapturing its original meaning and purpose. It is a Church rededicated to Christ's commission to proclaim the good news, to live it as a community, and to bear witness to it through generous service to the world's suffering people.

How Important Is the Bible?

Imagine reading an important book under a phosphorescent lamp to discover, between the lines, a previously unseen commentary on the text. This is similar to what has happened in recent years in the case of the Bible. Modern science has supplied biblical scholars with a new kind of light. The text remains the same, but the meaning has been illuminated in a marvelous new way.

Three modern sciences in particular have shed new light on the biblical text: language studies, history, and archaeology. Each of these sciences has matured only in the present century, and each has unlocked the biblical world in its own way.

About a century ago, the Bible was almost the only historical record of civilization previous to that of ancient Greece and Rome. All we knew of Mesopotamia, Babylonia, Assyria, Canaan and Egypt were the shreds of evidence scattered in the Bible. The situation changed dramatically when the ancient writing of the Middle East, such as hieroglyphics and cuneiform, were deciphered. Vast amounts of literature from these ancient civilizations were read for the first time since Old Testament days. As a result, the biblical narratives can now be placed within a massive background of information contemporary with the sacred books.

Important breakthroughs for biblical studies have occurred. The most valuable discovery has been the varied use of literary forms in biblical times. Just as we have such literary forms as the novel, poetry, and science fiction, ancient writers of the Middle East employed a variety of literary forms. Some of these forms have modern parallels; some of them do not. For example, the

Book of Jonah is very similar to a short story containing a mixture of fiction and history. The Book of Job is a dramatic dialogue, a play written for public reading rather than for acting. The history of the exodus as recorded in the early books of the Bible is a highly stylized and didactic kind of history without parallel in history books today.

Does this mean that certain biblical books do not record truth in a manner inspired by God? Certainly not. What it means is that we can now better understand what God is actually revealing through these sacred writings. God worked through many different authors. Each author wrote in a uniquely personal way. Each possessed his own abilities, historical concerns, and purpose for writing. It is wrong for us to assume that every author set out to write factually accurate history in the modern sense. Truth can be communicated in other ways. We now have abundant evidence that a wide variety of literary forms is used in the Bible. The key to unlock the inspired truth of each book is to know what specific literary form the author employs.

The science of history has also contributed greatly to a better understanding of the Bible. Many Old Testament events can now be accurately dated. Much of the political intrigue underlying Israel's troubled history has been unraveled and understood for the first time. For example, Egyptian documents confirm the exodus to have happened in the thirteenth century B.C., and Babylonian annals list the surrender of Jerusalem in approximately 597 B.C.

Finally, the science of archaeology continues to amass new data for biblical scholars. Ceramic chronology and carbon dating have uncovered layer upon layer of ancient Middle East life. Details of daily habits, utensils, ritual observances, and wars have been unearthed. From archaeological findings alone, enough material has been gleaned to document an entire history of the Holy Land from the time of Abraham to the time of Christ. Ancient settlements and trading routes mentioned in the Bible have been pinpointed.

The upshot of these modern scientific investigations is that our ability to read the Bible has been dramatically sharpened. As one Catholic scholar put it, more data concerning the Bible has been amassed in the past 50 years than in the preceding 18 centuries. Studied in the light of this new evidence, many biblical details can be better understood today than in the time of Saint Jerome and Saint Augustine, who were only a few centuries removed from the close of biblical days. Often enough, assumptions wrongly made because of inadequate background data have now been corrected. This applies to the New Testament as well as to the Old Testament.

All this may or may not sound exciting to the average adult Catholic. After all, few adult Catholics read the Bible or know much about it. On the face of it, the fact that bibli-

cal scholars are having a field day because of new scientific data is not likely to make a difference for the typical churchgoer.

It should make a difference, however. For one thing, Catholic children today are being taught to love and appreciate the Bible — and yes, to read it! For another, the revised scriptural readings at liturgical celebrations indicate the Church's intention to make the Bible more prominent in Catholic life.

How did it happen that generations of Catholics grew up with scant famil-

The truths of the Bible illuminate the Church's faith in every age

iarity with the Bible? Once again, the reason is traceable to the post-Reformation crisis in the Church. Luther and other reformers insisted that the Bible is the only source of divine revelation. The Catholic Church reacted by insisting, just as strongly, that sacred tradition is also a source of divine revelation. In the centuries that followed, Catholic education increasingly stressed sacred tradition much more than it stressed the Bible. By the time the Baltimore catechism came on the scene, sacred tradition had begun to dominate religion teaching almost completely. The Bible is hardly mentioned in the Baltimore catechism.

But the new stress on the Bible is not merely an effort to regain a lost balance in religious education. Theologians have discovered an important difference in approach to Christian teaching between the biblical message and post-Reformation catechisms. As we saw in the second chapter, there are different starting points and different priorities in each case. Experts agree that the biblical presentation is more authentic and more meaningful for man today.

How important is the Bible? It remains, as Catholics have always been taught, the inspired word of God. In the pages of this book is found a truthful and unfailingly accurate record of salvation history during its foundational periods. The truths of the Bible illuminate the Church's faith in every age: "All Scripture is inspired of God and is useful for teaching — for reproof, correction, and training in holiness so that the man of God may be fully competent and equipped for every good work" (2 Timothy 3:16-17).

Religious education today is bent on taking the above text out of the category of lip service and putting it into practice. With the aid of modern science, Scripture scholars have made the inspired message more accessible than ever before. Under the guidance of the teaching office of the Church, hopefully, Catholics, for the first time in centuries, will soon grow strong on the word of God.

Is Sacred Tradition a Thing of the Past?

Tradition is not a very popular word these days, especially among the young. Tradition smacks of unwillingness to get with the cultural revolution exploding all around us. But I suspect that most of us would subscribe to the wisdom of the song "Tradition" in *Fiddler on the Roof*: tradition is what helps us keep our balance. Without it, any organization would quickly fall apart.

For most adult Catholics, sacred tradition carries a hallowed meaning. Along with sacred Scripture, tradition is a font of divine revelation. It links the Church today with its historical beginning, providing a much needed sense of balance as we ponder the Church's future. And because the Church's future is the burning issue of the day, it is essential to know what sacred tradition means.

When the last of the twelve apostles died, the infant Church — a Church no longer connected to the historical Jesus through living witnesses — faced a new era. The Church had to keep the revelation of Jesus intact, as it had been handed on by the apostles. In some real sense, nothing could be added to or subtracted from the testimony of the apostles concerning Jesus. In short, the Church became aware of the importance of tradition.

Centuries passed in the life of the Church. But oddly enough, theologians rarely concerned themselves with the question: precisely what is tradition? Sacred tradition, like the Bible, was something pretty much taken for granted. The meaning of what God revealed through Jesus Christ was to be found in traditional understandings of the Church, especially those solemnly defined at ecumenical councils.

In practice, the Church, to test the truth of an idea, did not limit its sources to the Bible. Churchmen also resorted to the works of early Christian writers of high repute. If early bishops and theologians held a doctrine to be a part of Christ's revelation to the apostles, then its authenticity was accepted. After all, the Church had thrived for many years before the New Testament was

composed. Saint John's gospel states openly that the whole of Christ's revelation is not contained in writing:

> There are still many other things that Jesus did, yet if they were written about in detail, I doubt there would be room enough in the entire world to hold the books to record them.
>
> (John 21:25)

In other words, a source other than the Bible was recognized and used to determine the fullness of Christ's revelation.

At the time of the Protestant Reformation, this second source of Christian revelation came to be called sacred tradition. When Martin Luther rejected the authority of the pope, he was told that he was flying in the face of the tradition of the Church. He replied by expounding his now famous theory that Scripture alone is the source of Christ's teaching. This caused Catholic theology to develop, in opposition to Luther's position, the so-called "two-source theory" of revelation.

The two-source theory is found in its most advanced form in theology texts prior to about 1950. It also underlies catechetical texts written before 1950. The two-source theory, therefore, influences the thinking of most adult Catholics today, especially their concept of divine revelation. As a result of the *Dogmatic Constitution on Divine Revelation* of Vatican II, however, the two-source theory is presently undergoing a major revision.

To grasp the revised notion of sacred tradition forwarded by Vatican II, we must first examine the basic meaning of the two-source theory. On the surface, it is simple. It holds that Christ's revelation is contained in two historical sources, the Bible and sacred tradition. The Bible constitutes written revelation, and sacred tradition constitutes oral revelation — that is, truths which were handed down from Christ and the apostles by word of mouth and not recorded in the pages of the New Testament. By examining the works of early Churchmen known for their orthodoxy, we can bring to light the oral revelation of Christ. This the Church does, under the infallible guidance of the Holy Spirit, whenever the well-being of the Church demands. For example, in reply to Luther's charge that papal supremacy is not clearly grounded in the Scriptures, the Church pointed to the clear testimony of sacred tradition.

One flaw in the two-source theory is that it presupposes all revelation to be verbal. The theory works fine, assuming that Christ and the apostles were wholly absorbed in teaching propositional truths. If we equate divine revelation with verbal statements, everything falls neatly into order. The truth of Christ is passed along from age to age something like a football, whole and entire. The teaching office of the Church determines the deeper implications of this truth, as well as its relevance to a given age.

We have seen in Chapter 3, however, that divine revelation is no longer thought of exclusively, or even primarily, in terms of propositional truths. First and foremost, divine revelation is the saving *action* of God, through His Son Jesus, as experienced in the life of the Church. The doctrine taught by Jesus to the apostles is an integral part of divine revelation. But so, too, is Christ's death, resurrection, and *continuing presence* in the Church. In its fullest sense, divine revelation is something happening at all times within the Church. The people of God experience it, both individually and as a whole; for each Christian possesses the Holy Spirit, together with all other members of the Church, and with them is directed to respond to His promptings. In addition to the formal teachings of the Church, this continuous action of the Holy Spirit on Christian people constitutes divine revelation.

The Fathers of Vatican II unhooked sacred tradition from the two-source theory by stating:

> Now what was handed on by the Apostles includes everything which contributes toward the holiness of life and increase in faith of the People of God; and so the Church, in her teaching, life and worship, perpetuates and hands on to all generations all that she herself is, all that she believes.
>
> (*Dogmatic Constitution on Divine Revelation*, article 8)

Sacred tradition is not to be confined to the oral teachings of the apostles. In a larger sense, it also embraces the ongoing experience of the Church.

Nor does sacred tradition confine itself to the teaching office of the Church. It is experienced by the people of God as a whole. For this reason, Vatican II summons the laity to more active involvement in the life of the Church. The hierarchy retains responsibility to decide, in critical matters pertaining to the whole Church, what the Holy Spirit is or is not prompting the Church to say or do. But in arriving at this decision, the teaching office of the Church must listen to the testimony

Tradition is what helps us keep our balance

of the Catholic people, and not follow an ivory-tower approach.

Is sacred tradition a thing of the past? The answer is yes, if by tradition one means a backlog of verbal truths filed away in Vatican libraries. But if one means the accumulated experience of the Christian people, or the Church's living response to the gospel through the ages, the answer is definitely no. For, in this sense, tradition gives the Church stability. As it stands in the present, scanning the future, the Church finds in sacred tradition the means to keep its balance.

7

Papal Infallibility: Who? When? Where? How?

Every Catholic knows that his Church claims the divine guarantee of infallibility. Protestants, too, are aware that the Catholic Church makes this claim. Yet both Catholics and Protestants are too frequently unable to explain the exact meaning of infallibility.

In some obvious sense, infallibility means not to make a mistake. But what does this refer to in Catholic belief? How does it operate? What does it include? How did this doctrine originate? Is it grounded in reason? Such are the questions which Catholic teachers and parents should be able to answer.

The idea of infallibility was born with the Church itself. From the beginning, Christians believed that Christ and the gospel were permanently wedded to human history. The Sinai covenant was temporary; the new covenant of Christ is everlasting, a fact recalled at every Mass. Jesus promised to return visibly at the end of time, after His gospel has been preached to every creature. Therefore, the gospel will not undergo corruption nor be falsified in the course of history.

Saint Matthew's gospel (16:13-19) tells us that Peter plays a central role in the preservation of Christianity. Some Protestants argue that this passage applies to Peter alone. But the case for including Peter's successors is strong. Here Christ is promising that His Church will never fail. By himself, Peter could be the ground of this guarantee only so long as he lived. Clearly, Peter's successors would have to be the rock of the Church's stability after his death.

Other non-Catholics theorize that this passage was inserted years after Matthew's gospel had been completed, in order to bolster Roman pretensions to supremacy in the Church. There is no real evidence to support this theory, unless one arbitrarily assumes that Jesus did not intend Peter's office to be central in the Church. Again, it is argued that the original Greek text makes a distinction between Peter and the rock upon which the Church is founded. This argument supposes that the rock refers to Christ Himself. But this theory plays havoc with the known evidence.

In the first place, scholars widely agree that Matthew's gospel was first written in Aramaic, a Hebrew dialect, not in Greek. The Greek translator was forced to distinguish the word *petros* (Peter) from the word *petra* (rock), because in Greek, one term is masculine and the other is feminine. But in Aramaic, the two words are both masculine, and thus would be identical in the original text. Moreover, Saint John pointedly says in his gospel (1:42) that Jesus changed Peter's name from Simon, his given name, to Peter (rock). Here John provides background for the passage in Matthew, which had been written earlier. Simon was renamed Peter because on him was to fall the task of unifying and safeguarding the Church.

What can we learn from the facts of history? Unfortunately, the first century of the Church's history is poorly documented. From the shreds of evidence available, one can argue either for or against the supremacy of the bishop of Rome. We do know this: from the second century onward, the bishop of Rome has, in fact, been regarded as the head of the Church. Disputes have been referred to him for settlement. Councils have submitted their deliberations to the pope for approval. This procedure could hardly have won acceptance unless it had been viewed from the beginning as intended by Christ for His Church.

The case for the supreme authority of the pope is, therefore, quite strong. But strange to say, the doctrine of papal infallibility was not defined until the nineteenth century, at the First Vatican Council. Historically, the reason is that sometimes there was tension between popes and councils over how infallibility is supposed to work. The fact of infallibility was never in question. Solemn pronouncements of Church councils were held to be infallible by popes and bishops. But precisely to whom infallibility belongs, and under what circumstances it is to be exercised, remained partially obscure until the First Vatican Council.

Since the doctrine of infallibility was defined, about a century ago, most Catholics have known its essential meaning. In a unique way, infallibility belongs personally to the pope. No matter who or how many people say otherwise, a teaching cannot be called infallible unless the pope himself declares it to be so. Further, the pope must fulfill exacting conditions in order to make an infallible pronouncement. He must speak on a matter which, of its very nature, vitally affects the life and faith of the universal Church. He must address his statement to all members of the Church. Finally, he must openly declare that he is teaching infallibly.

These conditions must be taken seriously. Unless all are met, the pope is not acting infallibly. In the past hundred years, there were but two occasions when infallibility was exercised: when Pius IX defined the doctrine of the Immaculate Conception, and when Pius XII defined the dogma of the Assumption of Mary.

In practice, the power of infallibility works something like the power of the Congress of the United States to make constitutional amendments. While always there, it is seldom invoked. In his day-to-day work, the pope is fallible, confronting the same uncertainty and interplay of opposing points of view that characterize all human endeavor. Despite the guidance of revealed truth and the grace of the Holy Spirit, the pope can and does make mistakes.

Sometimes the doctrine of infallibility is extended far beyond the

> **In the past hundred years, there were but two occasions when infallibility was exercised**

limits of its exact meaning. For example, many Catholics falsely assume that Pope Paul's encyclical against birth control, *Humanae Vitae*, is an infallible document. They are, therefore, upset with theologians who disagree with the pope's position. At the time his encyclical was issued, however, Pope Paul VI made it clear that he did not intend it to be infallible. It is true that the Holy Father deserves a careful hearing from all,

and that, in forming one's conscience on this delicate matter, every Catholic must take into account what the pope has said. Yet it is equally true that the issue is not closed, once and for all. The pope chose to leave the door open to further speculation, and theologians who enter that door should not be condemned.

Is the question of infallibility settled, once and for all? Not entirely. We are certain of the conditions required for the pope to speak infallibly, but we are not certain of the human and the historical process which underlies the use of infallibility. In championing the idea of collegiality, Vatican II strongly suggests that the pope ought to consult his fellow bishops, and have their support, before making an infallible pronouncement. Ideally, the pope should simply declare, or make explicit, what the Holy Spirit has been bringing to consciousness in the people of God as a whole. In other words, revealed truth rises from the faith experience of the Church as a whole, not from the pope alone.

In short, infallibility does not lessen the fact that the Church is a mystery. It will remain so until the end of time. Christ did not guarantee that His followers would be free of doubt, or that His Church would make no mistakes in its operation. But He did guarantee that He would be with His Church always, and that the gospel would never be lost or hopelessly corrupted. The doctrine of infallibility is a necessary aspect of this guarantee.

8

Can the Church's Teaching Change?

Pressure is felt in the Church today for changes of all kinds. The age-old rite of the Mass has been changed. So, too, have the traditional garb and cloistered life-style of many sisters. Priest senates and parish councils have ushered in new forms of authority in the Church. We hear of speculation about clergy marrying and about bishops being elected for a period of years. What in the world is happening to the faith of our fathers?

Beneath the surface changes in the Church is a deeper concern, one which we must face squarely. Can the teachings of the Church undergo change? The question is important precisely because so many Catholics have the idea that the Church is a changeless monolith, an oasis of stability amid the shifting sands of time.

Not long ago, religion texts deliberately created the impression that Church teaching cannot change. A central idea was that divine revelation reached its completion with the coming of Christ. According to this notion, all the Church does in the course of time is to apply the truths revealed by Christ, as well as to draw out their fuller implications. Thus, dogmatic pronouncements of popes and ecumenical councils offer nothing really new to the original deposit of faith. They merely make explicit what was contained in the teachings of the apostles from the beginning.

To grasp the meaning of change in the Church today, some careful distinctions, as well as a sense of historical perspective, are necessary.

We may begin by considering why adult Catholics have been taught to have an aversion for changes in the Church. The historical reason is to be found in the crisis of Modernism. As we saw earlier, Modernism was a doctrinal battle which gripped the Church at the start of the twentieth

century. The crisis arose because of changes experienced in Western civilization by the advance of modern science and technology. As modern man became increasingly literate, mobile, and dynamic in his world view, tension mounted in the field of theology. Religious belief and practice, dressed in the garments of a bygone culture, seemed to lose credibility.

Many theologians began to seek a radically new expression for traditional Christianity. They tried to

After the condemnation of Modernism, a backlash occurred in the Church

preserve the essence of Christian faith, while updating its meaning for modern man in a way acceptable to modern science. Unfortunately, too many theologians failed. Some went so far to accommodate the intellectuals of the day that they washed out essentials of Catholic belief. As a consequence, in 1907, Saint Pius X resoundingly condemned the errors of Modernism.

After the condemnation of Modernism, a backlash occurred in the Church. Any theologian who did not uphold the traditional forms of Christian teaching became suspect.

This situation continued throughout the first half of the present century. Theology was in a kind of deep freeze of conservatism until the present renewal in theology got underway. Now that Vatican II has espoused the modern theological movement, a new era has decidedly dawned for the Church. Without hesitation, the task of squaring solid Christian understanding with solid scientific knowledge is being embraced.

Current religion texts reflect, perhaps all too accurately, the fact that theology today is immersed in the business of bringing about needed changes in the Church. The logjam created by the Modernist crisis was broken by the Second Vatican Council. The no-change mentality, ingrained by religion books of the past, is being swept away in the tide. To sort out the debris, we must carefully distinguish between what is subject to change and what is not.

First, there is real truth in the statement that divine revelation ended with the death of the last apostle, the last historical witness to the words and deeds of Christ. This historical witness of the apostles constitutes the climax of verbal revelation. Ever after, the core teachings of the gospel have remained fixed and are decisive in the Church's life. Apostolic teaching forms the deposit of faith in the strict sense and can never change.

On the other hand, we saw in the third chapter that divine revelation is not limited to verbal formulations. This fact, affirmed in the *Dogmatic Constitution on Divine Revelation* of Vatican II, is a major rediscovery for theology. It used to be widely assumed that all revelation comes to us in propositional form. Now, however, the Church has returned to an earlier, more balanced notion of revelation. The person of Jesus Christ is the heart of divine revelation. This person is living and active in the Church at all times. The action of Jesus Christ upon the people of God is something ever fresh, creative, and unpredictable. To the same extent that

> **At the heart of today's crisis in the Church is a changing attitude toward change itself**

the Holy Spirit continually renews the Church, divine revelation continues to expand.

There is, then, an unchanging core of divine revelation: the gospel handed on to us by the apostolic Church. But as the Church lives out the gospel in response to Christ and to His Spirit, divine revelation is constantly taking on new and unexpected meanings. Every epoch presents its own cultural outlook, world view, and set of values. The

Church is continually challenged to express the unchanging gospel in keeping with changing historical conditions: "Indeed, this accommodated preaching of the revealed Word ought to remain the law of all evangelization" (*Pastoral Constitution on the Church in the Modern World*, article 44).

We cannot assume that the Church in the past has expressed the meaning of the gospel in some timeless fashion or in a language that never grows old. In any given period of history, the teaching office of the Church shares the mental limitations and the vocabulary of the cultural continuum of the day. While infallibility guarantees a truthful statement of divine revelation, it does not guarantee that the cultural continuum employed in each case is relevant for all future ages. Neither does infallibility guarantee that the Church makes the best possible use of the verbal tools accessible to it for expressing divine truth.

At the heart of today's crisis in the Church is a changing attitude toward change itself. A generation ago, because of the heresy of Modernism, changes of any kind were considered to be out of the question. But people attuned to the mind of Vatican II have now abandoned that entrenched position. The Church's life and teaching have undergone much change in past centuries. Much change is called for today. We cannot be true to the gospel nor to the Spirit of Christ unless we respond to this call.

9

Can We Believe in Evolution?

Not long ago, I received a letter from a distraught father. His daughter had brought home a copy of HI-TIME, a weekly high school religion text, in which I had discussed the meaning of the creation narrative in Genesis. He wrote:

> Father, I will go to my grave believing, as I always have, that God created the world in six days, no more and no less, exactly as the Bible says.

I sympathize with this man and respect his feelings. He grew up in a time, not far removed, when the theory of evolution was flatly rejected in Catholic circles. As a matter of fact, my seminary college education took place during this time. My religion teacher all but stood on his head trying to show how the biblical account of creation makes sense when taken literally.

When I began to study theology, however, I discovered that evolution was accepted by some theologians as a working hypothesis. Now, almost 20 years later, there is scarcely a theologian who does not interpret the creation account in the light of the theory of evolution.

Why this about-face? To begin, we must understand why evolution seemed so threatening to Catholics a generation ago. The reasons can be reduced to two. First, prior to the modern biblical movement, it was customary to take everything in Scripture more or less literally. It was assumed that the authors of Genesis intended to document, in an historical and scientific fashion, the origin of the universe.

We know now that the first 11 chapters of Genesis, intended as a preface, were written several centuries after the rest of the book. Old Testament history actually starts with chapter 12, the account of Abraham, the progenitor of the Israelite people. Late in Israel's history, probably in the sixth century B.C., the question arose: What took place before Abraham? By this time the Jewish faith was quite mature. Throughout the nation it was believed that their God, Yahweh, was

> **The creation account can be reconciled with the theory of evolution**

the only God, and that all the world came from Him and was sustained by Him. Consequently, the authors of the creation account wished to assert this belief.

There is a second reason behind the rejection of evolution a generation ago. This, once again, is the crisis of Modernism. The first attempt of Catholic theology to integrate traditional belief with the theory of evolution ended in disaster. The condemnations of Modernism issued by Rome in 1907 effectively closed the door to speculation based on evolutionism. This held true until

roughly 1950. By then, modern biblical studies approved by Pius XII had progressed enough to show that the creation account can be reconciled with the theory of evolution. In the meantime, and for some years to follow, religion texts continued to denounce evolution as opposed to the Bible.

Now let us reconstruct the creation account as recorded in the first two chapters of Genesis. We noted that the authors intended to affirm the fact that Yahweh had created all things. Furthermore, in opposition to some pagan theories, they wanted to state that everything without exception came forth thoroughly good from the hand of God. It was unthinkable that the all-good and loving Yahweh could be the author of evil.

The writing technique, or literary form, chosen by the authors is both simple and imaginative. They depict God as a Jewish carpenter setting about the task of building the world. He labors for a full working week, six days, and rests on the Sabbath. His work is confined to daylight. Each evening, before quitting, He takes pleasure in the day's accomplishment: "God saw how good it was" (Genesis 1:12).

The logistics of the creation story parallel the popular understanding of the physical universe in ancient times. This concept was based solely on appearances. The earth itself is viewed as the center of the cosmos. Sun, moon, and stars are but furnishings for the earth. Further, the earth is conceived of as flat. Ocean tides are checked by no force other than the express command of God. The sky, touching all four horizons, is viewed as an inverted blue bowl resting on the earth's surface. It is supported by a substance termed firmament, which keeps the sky in place. Rain is explained as waters above the sky, waters which fell whenever God chose to open the floodgates.

A particularly interesting feature of the creation narrative is that light

Christian belief and scientific understanding are mutually supporting

is created on the first day (Genesis 1:3), whereas the sun is created only on the third day (Genesis 1:14-16). This reflects an ancient notion that sun and light are two distinct entities. Since light appears before the morning sun and persists after sundown, the two were thought to be causally independent.

The creation of man is given the climactic position in the narrative as if the first five days are meant to set the stage for what will follow. When all is in readiness, man ascends the stage as the central actor and the focal point of all creation. Thus,

the authors affirm that man is superior to the rest of creatures and that all else is for his benefit.

The biblical authors' theories about the universe may be quaint, but we are not to let them distract us from the true message. What the authors are saying is that Yahweh, the one true God, created the whole world, and everything in it is good. This is the truth which the authors affirm and, therefore, is the truth divinely revealed by sacred Scripture.

Today, then, we have learned to distinguish between what the biblical writers affirm to be true and how they communicate this affirmation. The authors of Genesis 1-2 do not theorize about the scientific nature of the universe. Rather, they simply use the prevailing notions of the world in order to detail their conviction that Yahweh is responsible for the world's existence. They make no stand for or against evolution; the question could not possibly have crossed their minds. Nor do they go on record in support of their personal theory of world physics.

In recent years the theory of evolution has taken a firm hold both in scientific and in popular understanding. There is nothing in the Bible to oppose this view of the world. Christian belief and scientific understanding are mutually supporting rather than contradictory. For this reason it is not only permissible to present Christian teaching in harmony with evolution; it is the only sound procedure.

10

Is Original Sin a Myth?

For generations of Catholics, the biblical narrative of Adam and Eve has been the one Old Testament passage familiar to everyone. There is good reason. How is one to explain the absolute necessity of salvation as a gift from God? Why can't a person make it on his own? Why is it that the history of nations, as well as of individuals, time and again, shows a deep-seated perverseness of some kind — an ingrained attraction to evil? The answer to these important questions has been simple: original sin.

But lately one hears strange things about original sin; the traditional notion has somehow been wrong; new evidence forces the Church to revise former understanding. So the talk goes.

A famous incident in the life of Mark Twain has some bearing here. Once when he visited in England, word spread in America that Twain had died. Hearing about it, Twain sent home the message: "The reports of my death are greatly exaggerated." The same can be said of much misguided talk about original sin.

We have seen that the theory of evolution can be reconciled with the creation account in Genesis. Two facts commonly agreed upon by biblical scholars help in this reconciliation. First, chapters 1-11 of Genesis were written much later than they were previously thought to have been, that is, toward the end of the period of Old Testament composition. Second, the authors were not writing history in the modern sense. They were theologizing about the origins of the cosmos.

The same insights apply to the Adam and Eve narrative. In accord with the soundest available evidence, the fall of our first parents is not set forth as historical reporting. Rather, the biblical authors are stating their convictions about the origin of evil, and man's unqualified need for redemption from God. These statements form a part of the inspired word of God, the Bible. What the authors of Genesis say, then, cannot be regarded as mere theory. They state the truth.

But precisely what are the authors telling us? If they do not intend to write history in the strict sense, what is their intention?

Let's try to reconstruct the situation faced by the biblical writers. They are Jewish scholars of deep faith. They believe that Yahweh, the God of their fathers, is the only real

God. All creation has sprung forth from His hand. They also believe Yahweh to be totally good, totally loving in His intentions toward man. Having insisted that Yahweh made all things good, these scholars confront a towering dilemma. What about the problem of evil? If God is in no way the source of hatred, greed, violence, and lust, then where do they come from? The question is not a matter of idle speculation.

About the time that the biblical authors were pondering the source of evil, Israel experienced the greatest crisis in her history, the Babylonian exile. Solomon's temple, God's earthly dwelling place, had been leveled by pagan hoards. All but a handful of no-accounts were dragged off in chains to Babylon. For all practical purposes, the promised land ceased to exist. Even the most devout Jew was tempted to dismiss his faith as a mythical romance with a nonexistent God.

But during her captivity Israel's faith miraculously revived. When, some 50 years later, Israel was permitted to return to her homeland, the Jewish faith blossomed forth as it never had before. The difference lay in the people's sensing their utter dependence upon Yahweh. They had come to realize that insofar as they were faithful to Yahweh, their fortunes would prosper. They could not possibly make it on their own. This was true regarding personal sin and evil, too; Yahweh alone could save man from his sinful condition. A God-sent savior would have to come,

bringing man a power for good that he could not possibly muster on his own.

Pondering these convictions, the authors of the Adam and Eve account affirm that man is himself responsible for evil, and that man is powerless to heal the ravages of personal and social sin. Like a cancer, evil has grown from its historical source, contaminating everything in its path.

"Adam" in Hebrew means "man," usually in a generic sense. "Eve" means simply "living." Today we would say that Adam and Eve are personifications of mankind at its origin. The biblical writers state that evil entered creation through the abuse of man's freedom. The story form employed, the snake and the tree of the knowledge of good and evil, are borrowed from pagan literature. The authors are not verifying the details of the story. They simply use the story to communicate, in a graphic way, their conviction that evil befell man in his origins because he disobeyed his Creator in some radical way. This is what they affirm; this is what biblical inspiration guarantees to be true.

What about Church doctrine concerning original sin? The main lines of the traditional doctrine of original sin were not formulated until the time of Saint Augustine in the late fourth and early fifth centuries. There were two pressing concerns at the time. One was the question of whether infants ought to be baptized, since they could not consciously respond to what Baptism is intended to be. The other concern was a heresy called Pelagianism, which viewed man as wholly good and capable of attaining salvation by his own efforts. In response to these problems, the Church insisted that Baptism effects a saving relationship with God in infants and that no man can be saved unless he is renewed inwardly by the power of Jesus Christ. In both of these teachings, the underlying problem the Church is addressing is original sin.

In the sixteenth century the Council of Trent again emphasized the

> Evil befell man in his origins because he disobeyed his Creator in some radical way

reality of original sin. Countering the naive optimism of some Renaissance humanists, the Council Fathers defined that original sin is a concrete reality in man, and that it must be eradicated through God's saving power if one is to enter eternal life. While affirming that original sin is transmitted through the human race from our first parents, the Council Fathers did not sanction Augustine's gloomy notion that this transmission is to be ascribed to the act of procreation.

Unfortunately, in popular understanding, the official statements concerning original sin became wedded to a literal interpretation of the Adam and Eve account. This is why so many feel threatened today when they hear that the Genesis narrative contains symbolic elements.

An updated understanding of original sin opens new questions, especially when one thinks within the framework of evolution. Speculation about when, how, and under what circumstances *homo sapiens* emerged from earlier forms introduces fascinating possibilities about the historical nature of original sin. While we can be open to these inquiries and have no fear of them, we can hold fast in faith to the basic revelation concerning original sin.

The bishops of Vatican II summarized the meaning of original sin in this way:

> . . . from the very beginning of his history man abused his liberty, at the urging of the Evil One . . . all of human life, whether individual or collective, shows itself to be a dramatic struggle between good and evil, between light and darkness. Indeed, man finds that by himself he is incapable of battling the assaults of evil successfully, so that everyone feels as though he is bound by chains. But the Lord Himself came to free and strengthen man, renewing him inwardly. . . .

(*Pastoral Constitution on the Church in the Modern World,* article 13)

11

Is Anything a Sin Anymore?

Sin is one of the more confusing topics we hear about these days. It is said repeatedly that Christian morality is essentially a matter of love, a fact we have always known. We are disturbed to learn that Catholics, old and young, are not flocking to confession as they used to. There is talk of an elastic type of morality, wherein each person decides for himself what is right or wrong.

For one reared in traditional moral teaching, the scene is frightening. We older Christians were not perfect in the past. But at least we knew where we stood. We knew the Commandments. We knew what is a mortal sin and what is a venial sin. And we knew we were sinners. Today it sometimes seems that nothing is clearly sinful.

What happened to the traditional ideas about sin? In a word, the traditional teaching has been discovered to be too one-sided. It stressed

one important aspect of Christian morality while neglecting another. The confusion experienced today in this sector of Christian understanding is a painful but necessary process of seeking equilibrium. We are trying to recapture the New Testament's balanced view of morality which thrived in the Church for centuries.

How did the balanced view of Christian morality become lost? Although it is a long and complicated story, we will put it briefly. After the Reformation, in reaction against Protestant teaching which tended to play down man's responsibility before God, Catholics overemphasized man's role in the process of salvation. But Luther and Calvin held that man is a sinner to the core, and that Baptism does not change this fact. According to them, salvation is a sheer gift from God; man cannot merit it by his good works. In response, the Council of Trent declared both that Baptism renews man inwardly, and that man is morally responsible to preserve baptismal grace in order to enter heaven.

This doctrinal dispute between Protestants and Catholics framed the moral teaching of the Baltimore catechism and similar texts. The whole thrust of the Baltimore catechism is upon man's personal responsibility to gain heaven. The Creed is presented as truths meant to enlighten man's conscience, giving him the necessary motives and intellectual orientation to live a life pleasing to God. The Commandments form the heart of the Christian message. From the Commandments one learns, in black-and-white certainties, what actions are to be done and which are to be avoided if one is to be saved. Finally, the sacraments are presented as sources of supernatural strength for avoiding sin and keeping the Commandments.

What is missing in this shaping of the Christian message? There is missing precisely what Protestantism was insisting on, to the neglect of legitimate Catholic concern. Strictly speaking, salvation is a free gift from God. Man does not earn heaven by good conduct. These statements are to be found in Church teaching as far back as the days of Saint Augustine, in condemnations of the heresy known as Pelagianism.

Are we then involved in a contradiction? How can the Church teach at one and the same time that salvation is totally God's free, unearned gift, and that man is nevertheless morally responsible before God — that he will be saved or condemned in accord with his conduct?

We must never forget that Christianity is a mystery. This is to say, the meaning of Christ and the gospel is not something that can be laid out piece by piece and logically assembled like a puzzle. We always remain in the position of believers. In faith we are committed to the teachings of the Church, not because they are inherently coercive to our minds, but because they are God's revelation. We cannot always comprehend what He reveals, but we can always trust His word as true.

Having said this, we hurry to add that a Christian mystery cannot contradict human reason. In other words, the two poles of Christian morality, God's role and man's role, can and must be reconciled in a way that makes sense. Let us see how the early Church handled this paradox.

Biblical morality insists loud and clear that salvation is God's gift to undeserving man. The gift par excellence is the person of Jesus Christ in His dying and rising on our behalf:

> I repeat, it is owing to his favor that salvation is yours through faith. This is not your own doing, it is God's gift; neither is it a reward for anything you have accomplished, so let no one pride himself on it.
>
> (Ephesians 2:8-9)

The gospel is good news for this very reason. Man does not have to save himself; in fact, he cannot. Rather, out of love and mercy, God has willed to do it Himself. The

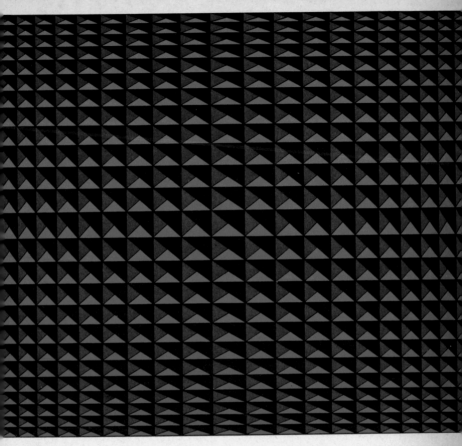

ground for our hope for eternal life is not our own moral integrity. It is the historical event of Christ's death and resurrection — something over which we have no control. Salvation is God's gift to all who accept it.

The Ten Commandments belong to Old Testament morality, and are rooted in natural morality. It is wrong, therefore, to look upon the Ten Commandments as the basis for Christian morality. The question of Christian morality cannot even arise until one knowingly and willingly accepts the loving Father's gift of salvation in Jesus Christ. This is not to say that the Ten Commandments have no place in a Christian's life. It is simply to say that one does not begin to live a Christian life until he is in a position to deal with the consequences of his free acceptance of the gift of redemption.

In an initial way, God's gift is received at Baptism, when one is transformed by insertion into Christ, sharing His Spirit — the Holy Spirit — as a new source of life. But in practice this initial transformation must be ratified as one grows to understand it. For a Christian moral conscience begins when one says yes to the Father's gift of Jesus Christ, and consciously affirms the work of the Holy Spirit in one's life.

At this point one begins to ask: What is the Holy Spirit doing in my life? How can I cooperate with His action? Putting it another way, how can I continue to say yes to the gift of redemption? In answer to this concern, one turns for guidance to the Ten Commandments and to other moral principles of Church teaching. Always, however, one's confidence for entering heaven rests on continuing openness to Christ, rather than on behavior conforming to legal norms.

Hand in hand with this fundamental biblical insight about Christian morality, modern psychology has shown traditional notions of mortal and venial sin to be too simplified and unrealistic. Supposedly, one could miss heaven just as certainly for omitting Mass on Sunday as for murder or grand larceny. It is misleading to absolutize mortal sin in this way. Mortal sin is a conscious severing of one's baptismal commitment. This is not done lightly or often. On the other hand, there are many shades of irresponsibility in a person's efforts to be true to his fundamental option as a Christian.

Sin is a continuing reality in a person's existence, and he must continually seek God's pardon. "It's only a venial sin" is the recourse of an immature legalist.

Again, sin is viewed not so much as an isolated act as a state of alienation, more or less serious, brought on by personal negligence before God. After all, human relations are measured much more by the quality of a person's enduring love than by single actions. The same is true in a person's relationship with God. He is not peering over the edges of heaven to mark when a person does this or that; His absorbing concern is a man's openness to His love and the man's response. While love without good works is empty, so too are good works without love.

Much more can be said. But the basic reason behind the new approach in teaching Christian morality and behind the sticky issues being raised about the meaning of sin is relatively simple. The Church is struggling to recapture the delicate balance in moral understanding of the gospel. For some time we have leaned too heavily in the direction of man's personal responsibility. While keeping this necessary perspective, we must open ourselves to the perspective uppermost in an earlier, more authentic tradition. Christ is our Saviour; we do not save ourselves.

12

Sanctifying Grace: Why All the Silence?

Check out any current religion text and, chances are, you will find few references to sanctifying grace. On the face of it, this silence is distressing. Sanctifying grace used to be a pillar of religious education. The state of grace, as opposed to the state of sin, dominated Catholic thinking on the sacraments and the moral life as a whole. Concern for sanctifying grace seemed the essence of Christian living.

Like clothes and architecture, vocabulary does not remain fixed. Read a Shakespearean play, or better still, a work of Chaucer, and the point is immediately clear. In religious education today, we are witnessing the obsolescence of the inherited vocabulary of grace. New expressions are sought to better convey the faith reality underlying the traditional terms.

To identify the former vocabulary of grace with divine revelation is erroneous. The terms so familiar to us did not spring full-blown from the apostolic Church. Rather, like many other religious words, sanctifying grace is a term which dovetailed with the peculiar mentality, the cultural world view, of a certain historical age. The term best expressed a central facet of the gospel for that generation of Christians. Another age, having a different world view, attempts to express the same truth in a way better suited to its own mentality.

To understand the changing vocabulary of grace today, we must ask ourselves what the traditional terms really meant, and why they are no longer considered to be adequate.

The word "grace" is found in the Bible; the term "sanctifying grace" is not. We have been so conditioned by the latter term that we equate it with the biblical word "grace." For example, in the revised standard version of the Bible, when we read ". . . by grace you have been saved . . ." (Ephesians 2:8), we assume that Saint Paul means sanctifying grace. In fact, however, Paul knew nothing of our terminology. He uses "grace" pretty much as a synonym for "gift." In this passage, as in his other writings, Paul is not hinting obliquely at a later theology of grace. Instead, he is emphasizing the fact that salvation comes to us as a free, unmerited gift from God. This is quite a different matter.

Is there a biblical parallel to our traditional notion of grace? Yes, but the parallel is not found in the word "grace." It is found in New Testament expressions concerning the intimacy and union of life which we Christians share with God.

Saint John's gospel (15:1-6) describes our union with Christ's risen life in terms of a vine and its branches. Saint Paul models his explanation on the human body and its various members, all participating in the same life (1 Corinthians 12:12-27). The first letter of Peter (2:4-5) uses the simile of a temple, saying that we Christians are living stones for the one sanctifying work of Christ, who dwells within us.

The truth affirmed in these passages is that the one life of Jesus Christ, risen and forever alive, is now shared by all His followers, mysteriously uniting all Christians in the same Holy Spirit. From the beginning this truth has been a source of fascination for theologians. The early Church Fathers probed the idea, and offered new similes to clarify it. One such simile is that of an iron poker placed in fire. When taken out, the poker gives off heat and light, thus, sharing in the life of the fire. So it is with the Christian after Baptism.

The term "sanctifying grace" arose in the Middle Ages as an attempt to explain, in philosophical terms, the precise relationship between the baptized Christian and the divine life of God. Saint Thomas Aquinas insisted that man cannot enter into the life of God and remain truly human unless his nature undergoes a structural change. Sanctifying grace is an adapter which transforms human nature, making it possible for man to actually participate in the life of God Himself.

As time went on, the distinction between sanctifying grace and the divine life which it meant to illuminate became blurred. A pragmatic cast of mind, together with a world view that put a premium on static concepts, latched onto sanctifying grace as a most usable coinage for Christian education.

Unfortunately, "coinage" all too aptly describes how the Christian life was understood. In an age which exaggerated the role of meritorious works, sanctifying grace was regarded as a kind of heavenly currency. To possess this substance was to merit heaven. To lose it was to invite dam-

nation. The sacraments were thought of primarily as means to obtain this saving capital or to increase one's holdings, and virtuous acts were thought of as means of gaining dividends.

One edition of the Baltimore catechism reflects with deadly accuracy the concept of sanctifying grace as a thing. Milk bottles depict the Christian soul. A white bottle illustrates the soul filled with grace. A bottle with black marks shows the soul with venial sins. An empty bottle stands for a soul devoid of sanctifying grace.

What is objectionable in this whole approach to grace? For one thing, a study of history reveals that the term "sanctifying grace" has assumed

We are witnessing the obsolescence of the inherited vocabulary of grace

an importance it does not deserve. When used correctly, the term should be secondary to the far more important mystery of the divine indwelling. The focus ought to be on God's life in man, not on a philosophical term created to try to explain the mystery.

Second, and even more significant, today the emerging world view is decidedly person-centered as opposed to thing-centered. To describe the Christian life in mechanical, static, and impersonal concepts is to pose a needless barrier to the gospel for the contemporary mind. We do far better service to young people in particular by returning to the person-centered images of the New Testament. After all, our purpose in this area of Christian doctrine is to convey what the inspired writers themselves attempted to explain; namely, that Christ's Spirit is truly living in us and we in Him.

There is a third reason for the growing silence about sanctifying grace. The vocabulary of grace used in the past worked hand in hand with an idea of salvation called extrinsicism. Grace was viewed as coming to man from a world extrinsic to his experience. It was as if God worked from beyond the sky. Today this mind-set is generally rejected. The divine life breaks in upon us, like the incarnation itself, on the ground level of human experience, not from an upper story beyond our known world.

To look upon the life of grace as something extrinsic to life itself makes it seem superfluous and irrelevant. Today man is too absorbed in this life to concern himself with another. Man is designed to find completion in a community of life with God. All human experience points in this direction. To be Christian is to be authentically human. If our vocabulary of grace obscures this fact, we need to sharpen our vocabulary.

13

After Death, What Then?

In our time, there seems to be a conspiracy against death. The attention that used to be given to heaven, hell, and purgatory has faded from the scene. When people do talk about these things, it is usually in a guarded way and with a good deal of skepticism.

It is said that the very idea of hell runs counter to the goodness of God; therefore, hell probably does not exist. And if hell is to be consigned to the domain of Mother Goose, then heaven probably belongs there, too. Who really knows if anything happens beyond the grave? It seems best to make the most of the life we now have, and forget the rest. So run the thoughts of contemporary man.

Still, the stark reality of death is too much to ignore. What are we to make of the loss of persons we love? Do their lives have any further meaning? Is one who laughs and loves, who knows fear and heroism and haunting desire no different at last than a blighted flower? And if man is something more, if death is a doorway rather than a blind alley, what lies beyond? Can we prepare for it? If so, how?

The Christian answer to these persistent questions has not changed. Christ assures us that life is forever. Death will open onto heaven or hell, and both will go on everlastingly. Man's life beyond death will be determined by how he lives on this side of the grave.

It must be added, however, that some of the skepticism about heaven, hell, and purgatory is justified. The problem lies in childish, popular views of these realities. Divine revelation does not support the notion of heaven as a gigantic throne room where angels play harps and people endlessly sing psalms. There is nothing to substantiate the image of hell as a smoldering cauldron commandeered by devils armed with pitchforks. Biblical allusions to hellfire are metaphorical. That purgatory is a San Quentin adjoining the pearly gates is also a groundless theory.

These graphic images are inherited from an age that found them useful. For better or worse, the aim was to instill a dread of sin. Terror of hell gave strong motivation to walk the straight and narrow. The pains of hell were dramatized to create this pragmatic effect. In an age permeated with faith, this tack met with qualified success. The view of the gospel as the *good* news was obscured. People lived with a healthy fear of ending up in hell.

In the secular world of today, compounding dreadful images of hell no longer has the desired effect.

Instead of being frightened, people turn away from religion as an illusion. They dismiss the God-problem, and the question of death's meaning, as insoluble. They prefer to concentrate on the present life — which is complex and challenging enough to absorb them completely.

The situation forces us to return to the sources of divine revelation, and to carefully reassess the meaning of heaven, hell, and purgatory. What has been discovered by theologians is not really new. Yet the old truths are given fresh meaning — a meaning that makes sense to the modern mind.

The one thing we know for certain about heaven is that it is fullness of life lived in community. This life starts to unfold on earth. Through Baptism man enters mysteriously but truly into the triune life of the blessed Trinity. At the same time, his life is merged with the lives of countless others who form the people of God. On the conscious level, the Christian is called to love his fellowmen, to promote peace and harmony among others according to his personal capacity and circumstances. An enduring response to this divine call culminates, after death, in eternal life in the community of heaven.

The one thing we know for certain about hell is that it is a state of noncommunity. "The absence of God" is the phrase traditionally used to describe the essential pain of hell. But together with God's absence, one will experience the absence of loving people. Loneliness is another word for hell, which is self-imposed. One who says no to God's invitation to love in his lifetime will wake, beyond the grave, to live with that same no forever. God does not retaliate for a person's refusal to cooperate in life. He merely seals forever what the self-centered person has consciously made of himself.

Underlying the choices each person makes from day to day is a radical choice for either heaven or hell. This fundamental option, as theologians call it, orients all other choices we make. Like a row of falling dominoes, the pattern of our lives is directed by this root choice to love others or to use them for self-aggrandizement, to go out of ourselves in concern for others or to hole up in a shell of self-concern.

Purgatory enters the picture this way. A man who chooses to build community rather than walls of division is seldom very consistent. While his fundamental option remains constant, his performance does not. There are many infidelities along the way, some serious and some light. In other words, serious sin and venial sin are realities we all contend with. Mortal sin, however, touches on a reversal in our fundamental option — something that happens infrequently.

At the moment of death a person passes from the shadowy uncertainties and flickering insights of the present life into a state of total, unobscured truth. Instantly, the Father's loving purposes, the unfailing care of Christ, and the healing strength of the Holy Spirit will become overwhelmingly apparent in his personal history. To the extent that he has been unfaithful to God, this moment of recognition will be painful and purifying. This concept of purgatory is speculation, as are older concepts. Its advantage is that it makes better sense.

Our difficulty, of course, is that we are dealing with revealed truths concerning eternity. We have no experience of eternity. All our projections are framed within the continuum of space and time to which we are limited. Heaven is not "up," and hell is not "down," nor is purgatory for a measurable period of time. We use these terms only because we cannot conceive of accurate ones.

The particular judgment we envision at death will not be in a courtroom setting. We speak of Christ as judge only in limping analogy. Divine revelation suggests that our judgment is being forged day by day, in keeping with the fundamental option underlying our most casual choices. From this perspective, we shall actually pass judgment on ourselves by accepting the consequences of what we have freely chosen to become.

Death will be the moment of truth. In naked clarity we will see the real person our lives have made us. Either we shall be open to the union of life and love which is heaven, or we shall be closed up with the loneliness in ourselves which is hell. In either case, the verdict will flow from our basic stance toward the community of mankind now.

14

How Human is Christ?

The rock opera *Jesus Christ Superstar* is a source of aggravation to some Christians. The work portrays Christ on the eve of His death, wracked with doubt about the Father's will and with confusion about His personal identity. For people accustomed to thinking of Jesus first and foremost as the divine Son of God, it is shocking to see Him depicted as so utterly human.

The opera can be questioned on grounds of orthodoxy. It strips the Last Supper of its traditional sacramental meaning, and appears to ignore the issue of Jesus' divinity. From another viewpoint, the work handles Jesus' humanity more correctly than some overly pious religious books. In this opera Christ comes through as *really* human. People can easily sense His manhood, and identify with His personal struggles.

To think of Christ as an authentically human person, as genuinely human as ourselves, ought to come easily for us. But it does not. Though we believe Christ is true man, we instinctively put greater stress on the fact that He is true God. After all, being divine is greater than being human! The uniqueness of the man Jesus is that He alone is the Son of God.

Yet thinking of Christ is not an either-or proposition. It is not a question of preferring one of His two natures over the other. This is implicit heresy. Mature Christian understanding knows but one person in whom full manhood is integrated with true Godhead.

Historically, a part of the problem lies in the traditional notion of Jesus' human consciousness. How did Jesus'

human mind function in relation to His divine mind? In the past, it was theorized that, humanly, Jesus was always aware of His divine nature. Further, it was argued that, as man, Jesus always had at His disposal God's knowledge. This meant that He knew at any given moment His own future in detail. Further, He was in command of the thoughts of everyone around Him.

This theory has always created difficulties. The gospels indicate that Jesus' youth was normal: "Jesus, for his part, progressed steadily in wisdom and age and grace before God and men" (Luke 2:52). In His public life Jesus is described as professing ignorance at times, and as seeking information (Mark 5:30; 13:32).

If Jesus' human mind was always in immediate contact with the mind of God, as a child He did not really learn how to talk; as a man He did not really have need to pray, and He did not really mean it when He cried out on the cross, "My God, my God, why have you forsaken me?" (Mark 15:34). In short, the humanness of Jesus comes off as a kind of charade. The so-called human actions of Christ appear to be so dominated and predetermined by His divine nature that they hardly seem human at all.

An incident some years ago made me vividly aware of the shortcomings of the traditional explanation of Jesus' human consciousness. I was teaching a class on the humanness of Christ. A lad with a skeptical look raised his hand. "Aw, Jesus wasn't *really* like us," he ventured. "Jesus had it *made!* He always knew what was coming next, and knew He'd win out. Who else has life that easy?" The student had a point.

The epistle to the Hebrews answers the objection, though we seem reluctant to accept at face value what we read:

> Since he was himself tested through what he suffered, he is able to help those who are tempted (2:18).
> For we do not have a high priest who is unable to sympathize with our weakness, but one who was tempted in every way that we are, yet never sinned (4:15).
> Son though he was, he learned obedience from what he suffered . . . (5:8).

Yes, Jesus was — and is — really like us!

Today Scripture scholars widely agree that we have not been accustomed to taking Jesus' humanness as seriously as did the early Christians. For example, if you read Saint Peter's address on Pentecost Sunday (Acts 2:22-40), you will find that every mention of Jesus is in terms of His manhood. We tend to forget that the apostles only gradually came to recognize and affirm the divinity of Christ. Their absorbing concern was that this man from Nazareth had become God's instrument for the world's salvation. We must not forget that gospel passages affirming Christ's divinity were written 30 years and more after the resurrection, and testify to postresurrection faith about events that happened before the resurrection.

Today the question of Jesus' human consciousness is under intense study. Father Karl Rahner, one of the Church's leading theologians, suggests that Jesus grew up much more normally than we tend to suppose. Christ lived out the human condition to the full. An integral part of the human condition is to struggle with doubt and uncertainty. It makes sense to assume that Jesus evolved in self-understanding as the years went on, just as we do. Some theologians theorize that it was not until

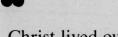

Christ lived out the human condition to the full

the resurrection that Jesus was at last completely aware of His identity as the Son of God.

This theory creates problems, too, especially in relation to our long-standing assumption that Jesus was always humanly attuned to divine knowledge. Still, the newer theory has advantages. It accords much better with the scriptural accounts of Jesus. It eliminates the charade problem: Jesus really did learn to talk, He really did feel an acute need to pray, and He really did feel abandoned during His passion.

Another advantage of the newer theory is that it enhances the meaning of the incarnation. Formerly, we thought of the incarnation as a necessary prelude to Christ's redemptive death and resurrection. Jesus' teaching and miracles were regarded as a conditioning process getting people ready for what Jesus knew was coming later. This view makes light of the incarnation. Christ's humanity is reduced to being a passive instrument of His divinity. As that student put it, Jesus does not come off as *really* being like us.

The incarnation means that the Son of God actually became one of us *in every respect except sin*; that is, Christ lived the human condition to the core of His being. He saved us, not only by dying and rising, but by confronting human life moment by moment, weathering small and great crises that arose from one day to the next. He was tempted. He experienced disappointment, frustration, and real loneliness.

Yet, He did not sin. To sin is to say no to the Father's will. Unfailingly, Jesus responded to His Father's invitation to spend Himself on behalf of His fellowmen. He gave His all to bring the kingdom of God into existence. Not once did He consciously back away from this challenge. But to build the kingdom of God is what human life is all about. Thus, Jesus was — and continues to be — the one fully authentic human being. He is the cause of our salvation because, of all men, He alone is truly a man.

15

Sacrifice of the Cross:
Why Did Christ Die?

No adult Catholic would deny that Christ's death on the cross is at the heart of God's plan of salvation. Old and young, conservative and progressive, would answer yes to the question in Luke 24:26: "Did not the Messiah have to undergo all this so as to enter into his glory?"

Yet today there is tension among Catholics over the exact role of Christ's cross in our redemption. This tension becomes clearest in connection with the Mass. Traditionally, the thought of the suffering Saviour permeated our outlook on the Mass. We defined the Mass as a sacrifice — a reenactment of the one sacrifice of Calvary. Fittingly, a large crucifix dominated the altar — the altar of sacrifice. An atmosphere of hushed silence, of heavy somberness, prevailed during the holy sacrifice.

Now look at what is happening. Guitars play. Songs are joyful and snappy. Banners and dialogue, friendly greetings, bright vestments, and a general air of relaxed informality have taken over. What in the world is going on?

We could cite the new liturgical directives which have issued from Rome in a steady stream since Vatican II. But this does not throw much light on why the liturgy has changed. Being told to celebrate Mass differently does not calm the fear of people who complain that they no longer can pray, and who feel somehow betrayed by the recent liturgical changes. For how can the passion and death of Christ be associated with the new festive liturgical spirit?

Two fundamental questions lie at the root of understanding why the liturgy has changed. First, what is the precise meaning of the redemptive sacrifice of Christ? Second, how is this meaning to be applied to the Mass?

These questions are intertwined, and are best approached by way of history. During the early centuries of the Church, the Mass was thought of dominantly as a celebration of the resurrection of Christ, in which His risen presence is encountered. The context was that of a community of believers gathered around a table and jointly engaged in prayerful response to His priestly action.

In the Middle Ages Christians gradually became more enamored by the theme of Christ's sacrificial death at Mass. This shift in focus from Christ risen to Christ dying had complex causes. Times were stern and arduous. In the face of the Black Death and the Hundred Years' War, the common man was much consoled by identifying with his crucified Saviour. Too, at this time people were singularly lacking in a sense of history. Even on the level of scholarship, there was little effort to understand the present by studying the past. Liturgical meanings suffered as a result.

Probably the greatest influence behind a growing fixation on the passion of Christ was the theory of sacrifice which prevailed in the Middle Ages. According to this theory, the physical shedding of Christ's blood was payment to divine justice for the debt of mankind's sins. Redemption was viewed in legal terms. A debt was incurred through sin and, by accepting His bloody death, the Son of God made fitting recompense for

this debt. Thus, in this theory, man's redemption was hinged to Christ's death; His resurrection was not the central issue.

The same "strict justice" theory of Christ's sacrifice held sway at the time of the Reformation. When Martin Luther lashed out against the empty ritualism of much liturgical practice, he went to the heart of the problem — as he saw it — by denying the sacrificial character of the

> **Today there is tension among Catholics over the exact role of Christ's cross in our redemption**

Mass. He held that the Mass is no more than a prayer form, and that only to the degree that genuine prayer is occasioned, does anything at all happen. The Council of Trent countered by solemnly defining that the Mass is a true sacrifice — the very sacrifice of Christ Himself.

From the sixteenth century until the Second Vatican Council, popular Catholic piety has been strongly conditioned by these events. First and foremost, the Mass has been understood as a sacrifice, and sacrifice itself has been understood according to the strict justice theory of the redemption.

In the past few years, changes in liturgical practice stem from a more enlightened and more balanced approach to the Mass. The Mass is a *sacrifice*, as Trent declared. But the Mass is more than a sacrifice. The controlling context of Eucharistic Celebration is that of the Last Supper: a *sacred meal* is taking place — among friends and with Christ. Christians are gathered to encounter Christ in faith: first in His word, then in the life of His risen person. This is done not in isolation, but in unison, by the active engagement of everyone present. The prevailing mood is not the sadness of Calvary, but the joy of Easter Sunday.

How, then, are we to explain the Mass as the sacrifice of Christ? Here we must let our legalistic notions yield to the New Testament idea of sacrifice. We have already seen that Christ's sacrificial action is not to be limited to His passion and death. The epistle to the Hebrews affirms that Christ's sacrifice began at the very moment of His incarnation:

Wherefore, on coming into the world,
Jesus said:
"Sacrifice and offering you did not desire,
but a body you have prepared for me;
Holocausts and sin offerings you took no delight in.
Then I said, 'As is written of me in the book,
I have come to do your will, O God.' "

(Hebrews 10: 5-7)

Christ's death on the cross was not the one moment of His sacrifice. Rather, it was the climactic moment, when His lifelong sacrifice surfaced most clearly. The essence of Christ's sacrifice lies not in the physical shedding of His blood, but in His selfless response to the will of His Father. The redeeming action of Christ — His sacrifice for us — stretches from the start of His human consciousness to the end. Yet this sacrifice is most magnificently revealed as He confronts death: " . . . not my will but yours be done" (Luke 22:42).

Strictly speaking, however, there has been no end to Christ's human consciousness, nor to His disposition to the Father's will: "Jesus Christ is the same yesterday, today, and forever" (Hebrews 13:8). Christ today relentlessly works to transform the fragmented human race into the one people of God, just as He did 2000 years ago in Palestine. At Mass Christ's word is spoken to us, and we feed on His risen life in order to sweep our lives upward into the same work. For the Father wills that we, too, infuse the world with the renewing power of the Holy Spirit. It is in this sense that the one sacrifice of Christ is re-presented, and that we are drawn into it.

The new form of celebrating Mass is, therefore, both timely and significant. The risen Lord is among us, teaching, healing, making us strong. This is reason to *celebrate*!

16

The Resurrection:
Past, Present or Future?

The keystone of Christianity is belief in the resurrection of Christ. Every other doctrine stands or falls with this one:

I handed on to you first of all what I myself received, that Christ died for our sins in accordance with the Scriptures; that he was buried and, in accordance with the Scriptures, rose on the third day; that he was seen by Cephas, then by the Twelve. After that he was seen by five hundred brothers at once, most of whom are still alive. . . .

(1 Corinthians 15:3-6)

These words of Saint Paul are the earliest historical record of the resurrection. In an almost casual way, the words explain why, some 20 years after Jesus' inglorious execution, a vibrant and irrepressible movement infected Palestine. This movement, known as Christianity, has continued growing ever since. Today it numbers countless thousands of followers in every nation of the world.

The first Christian teachers built their entire message on the resurrection of Christ. Everything else flowed from this. Paul's writings, while not ignoring Jesus' death, are saturated with the theme of Christ's resurrection. Every Eucharist celebrated in the early Church revolved around Christ risen and present in glory.

Theology in our time is marked

by efforts to reawaken all Christians to the centrality of the resurrection. For recent generations of Christians, the place of the resurrection in the mystery of redemption tended to be preempted by the sacrifice of the cross. We saw before why this happened. In defense of the sacrificial character of the Mass, popular piety was riveted on the theme of Christ's death. The cross was regarded as the prime moment of our redemption because, according to the strict justice theory, God's wrath for our sins was assuaged by the blood of Christ.

The most unfortunate aspect of this theory is that it gave the resurrection a backseat. The resurrection was viewed first as a personal reward to Christ for fulfilling His Father's will, and second as a proof to us that Christ is indeed the Son of God. Beyond this we found little meaning in the resurrection, other than the fact that it somehow guarantees our own resurrection at the end of time.

Presently, however, the Church is rediscovering the primacy of the resurrection in the mystery of man's salvation. We are returning to the understanding of the first Christians — that the reason we are a redeemed people is to be found first and foremost in the fact that Christ is risen.

The basic question is: What does it mean to be redeemed? Formerly, we would have answered something like this: To be redeemed is to possess sanctifying grace. Grace is something that transforms a sinner into a child of God. Grace comes to us from the sacraments, and ultimately derives from the merits which Christ gained by dying on the cross.

Without dealing with the above answer as such, we will simply note that the first Christians would have given a quite different reply. In Acts 2:14-39, we find a classic example — Saint Peter's discourse to the first converts on Pentecost Sunday. Four points are stressed. The very same four points are stressed repeatedly throughout the New Testament, and constitute the core of the gospel.

First, this man Jesus, known to have been dead, is now alive in a new and definitive way, having been raised to immortal life by God.

Second, the death and resurrection of Christ was decreed by God for the everlasting benefit of mankind.

Third, to obtain this benefit one must believe, repent, and be baptized.

What is this benefit? This is the fourth and final point of the good news. Those who open themselves to God through faith and Baptism receive Christ's Spirit and, thereby, are made co-sharers in His risen life.

To enter into Christ's Spirit — the Holy Spirit — is what salvation is really all about. It is the Holy Spirit who frees us from the bonds of sin and makes us God's children: "All who are led by the Spirit of God are sons of God" (Romans 8:14). It is the Holy Spirit who gives us superhuman strength to help rebuild the human race with Christ: " . . . the love of God has been poured out in our hearts through the Holy Spirit who has been given to us" (Romans 5:5). It is the Holy Spirit who assures us of eternal life:

> If the Spirit of him who raised Jesus from the dead dwells in you, then he who raised Christ from the dead will bring your mortal bodies to life also, through his Spirit dwelling in you.
>
> (Romans 8:11)

John the evangelist wants us to understand that throughout Jesus' earthly life He hungered to impart the Spirit of God to all men. This

We are returning to the understanding of the first Christians

same Spirit guided His conscious life from the moment of His baptism in the Jordan river. But it was only by dying that Jesus at last arrived at the moment He so longed for. Wakened from death, Jesus rose with the power to communicate the Holy Spirit to whomever He chose. This is the meaning of the biblical language concerning Jesus' ascension to the right hand of God,

and His claim to hold "full authority . . . both in heaven and on earth" (Matthew 28:18).

Does this approach to the mystery of redemption constitute a real difference for us? It definitely does. For one thing, this approach avoids abstractions like "merit," "grace," and "satisfaction for sin." Instead we are forced to think of salvation in highly personal terms: the Father's love, the life of Christ, and the power of the Holy Spirit within us.

A second difference lies in the relative importance given Christ's resurrection. We speak of it not mainly in the past tense, as an historical happening which shed light on Christ's death. Rather, we see Christ's resurrection as a timeless e v e n t dominating the history of salvation from start to finish. Christ not only rose; He is risen! Jesus not only lived; He is alive for us now — much more fully alive than before His resurrection.

But this is not all. As we say at each Mass, "Christ will come again!" For one attuned to the full meaning of the resurrection, *hope* is a chronic habit. One is incurably eager for the climax of what is now in process. Like a leaven, the power of Christ risen is at work in history, transforming men of goodwill everywhere into the one people of God.

What is the proper focus in time for the resurrection of Christ? It is not primarily the past, as we have too long tended to think. It is the present, with an eager eye to the future.

17

Sacraments:
Persons, Places or Things?

During the past 10 years, a quiet revolution has occurred in the Church's liturgy. True, there have been occasional complaints about guitar Masses and about too much talk from commentators; nevertheless, the average parish Mass today is amazingly different from the parish Masses of the past.

The remarkable thing is that there are not more complaints. After all, we Catholics are proud that our religion rests on an ancient heritage. We reject the notion of change for the sake of change. How, then, are we to explain the obvious and dramatic changes that have taken place in the Mass and in the sacraments?

The first point that ought to be made is that we are not really creating a new liturgy. When an institution is as ancient as the Catholic Church, a different approach is not necessarily a departure from tradition. It may be a return to an earlier tradition, more authentic than the one immediately preceding it. This is, in fact, the case with the new liturgy of the post-Vatican II Church.

The Mass and the sacraments, as we knew them a decade ago, followed a form dating back to about the fifteenth century. There were earlier forms of liturgical practice. The apostles had not celebrated Mass as the Renaissance popes celebrated it. Nor had Saint Augustine administered Confirmation exactly as Saint Francis de Sales administered it. The question we must ask is this: What prompts the Church to change the form of sacramental celebration from time to time?

Notice that we have been making a distinction between a sacrament as such, and the form by which a sacrament is administered. We are

not questioning the fact that there are true sacraments instituted by Christ. We are asking why sacraments are celebrated in different ways, at different times in the course of history.

Let us begin by asking what the form of a sacrament is, and what it is intended to do. The form is the perceptible part of a sacrament: the words and the actions. Ideally, the sacramental form makes known what is happening in the invisible realm of faith. Each of the sacraments places us in contact with God in a different way. The form of each sacrament prepares us for this contact, disposes us, and serves as the sensible medium for God's action.

All of the sacraments have one thing in common. They all constitute an encounter with Jesus Christ. Jesus Christ is the one and only Saviour. He is today, in an invisible way, what He was from the first moment of His incarnation. He is the revelation of God to men. The eternal, mysterious, and all-powerful God makes Himself known to man in only one way: through His Son, Jesus: " . . . no one knows the Father but the Son — and anyone to whom the Son wishes to reveal him" (Matthew 11:27).

Now that Jesus is risen, He is no longer seen in the flesh. Yet He remains in the Church at all times: "And know that I am with you always, until the end of the world!" (Matthew 28:20). Invisibly at work in the Church, Jesus, by means of sacraments, continues to reveal Himself to us in a tangible way, and thus continues to reveal the Father. In other words, the form of a sacrament is supposed to show, in a graphic way, how and why Christ is now entering our experience.

When Mass was celebrated in Latin, the sacramental form was unable to achieve its full purpose. The prayers and Bible readings are meant to open our understanding to Christ's present action. If the words are unintelligible, we cannot benefit or cooperate as we should. Being caught up in a sense of mystery is not enough. The rite is designed for our understand-

> **Each of the sacraments places us in contact with God in a different way**

ing. The rite calls for communal listening and response. It is not enough to read a translation. Community action is badly hampered when people are individually absorbed in reading a translation of what is going on. This is why the Mass and the sacraments are now celebrated in our native tongue.

Why, then, did the Church use Latin for so many years, even though people could not understand it? The main reason is found in the doctrinal controversy with Protestantism.

Martin Luther denied that sacraments are anything other than forms of prayer. Defending its tradition, the Catholic Church insisted that sacraments are clear signs of Christ's activity upon us. What man himself puts into sacramental celebration is small in comparison with Christ's action. Thus, while Protestants turned to the use of their native languages in order to "pray" the sacraments, the Catholic Church reaffirmed the validity of sacramental celebration in the Latin tongue.

The Second Vatican Council marked a thawing in the long controversy. The *Constitution on the Sacred Liturgy* called for a return

> " What really matters is people — people in need of Christ and alive to what He is doing "

to an earlier, more balanced tradition of sacramental practice. Once again, Catholics are invited to participate in the Mass and in the sacraments with an immediacy and understanding made possible by the use of their native languages.

But there is more to the contemporary renewal in the Church's liturgy. Not only have sacramental rites been translated into the vernacular; the rites have also been redesigned

to make better sense in the contemporary world. Chaucer's poetry is a form of English, but it is so dated that it is almost incomprehensible today. So it is with some aspects of sacramental form. To help us better perceive Christ's action, the Church has updated the form of the sacraments. We are all familiar with the new rite for the celebration of Mass. Similar new rites are now available for all the sacraments.

Finally, customs which influence the way that people use sacraments are also subject to change. Catholics today receive the Eucharist far more frequently than they did 50 years ago. The reverse is true for the sacrament of Penance; many Catholics now go to confession less than they did five or ten years ago. Again, many parishes now encourage the reception of First Holy Communion before first confession. An investigation of Church history would show that similar variations occurred many times over.

Today the Church invites us to shed preoccupations with legalistic and mechanical details, and to concentrate more on what sacraments are. They are not things, however sacred. Place and time are not of the essence. What really matters is *people* — people in need of Christ and alive to what He is doing. In each of the sacraments, Christ breaks into our consciousness in order to bring His strong love and healing power. We must be open to Christ's approach. Sacramental rites are designed to help us do just that.

18

Why Mass Every Sunday?

A few years back, when Friday abstinence was still Church law, a graduate of a Catholic college was being initiated into a Catholic organization. He was asked: What are the two most important requirements of our faith? Without batting an eye he replied: Not eating meat on Friday and going to Mass on Sunday.

In these post-Vatican II days, we may be tired of hearing about the double commandments which tower over our faith: to love God and to love our fellowmen. But at least we are more aware today of the primacy of love in Catholicism, and that is progress.

But many Catholics still tend to honor the law itself more than the good which the law is designed to promote. The third commandment is a case in point. What motivates people as they enter the doors of their parish church on Sunday morning? A tell-tale phrase frequently used is, to fulfill one's Sunday obligation. This motivation smacks of legalism. If one attends Mass primarily to observe a law, his faith is, at best, immature. He is like a child who obeys without understanding. In addition, an adult runs the risk of pharisaism. He may rest secure in his fidelity to the law, forgetting that salvation is a sheer gift flowing from Christ's death and resurrection — not from his personal obedience to law. The law is no more than a doorway through which God's gift is encountered. To trust in the law itself is to rest on the doorway without going in.

What lies beyond the doorway of the third commandment? This should be our central concern. It is the concern addressed by most modern religion texts. In an age that prizes freedom and personal fulfillment above every other value, no other approach to the third commandment is sound today. Happily, this pragmatic necessity is forcing all of us to purify our attitude toward Sunday Mass.

First, the law concerning Sunday Mass must be viewed within the larger context of the meaning of the gospel. In essence, the good news is that God freely chooses to save mankind in and through Jesus Christ. Man does not save himself — even by obeying the Commandments. Man has but to open himself, through faith, to the free gift of salvation. By being baptized, a person implicitly does this. He accepts the Holy Spirit, and undertakes a gradually deeper and ever more mature response to this gift.

Second, the purpose of Sunday Mass must be understood in light of the fundamental message of the gospel. To respond to the Holy Spirit is not always easy. Immersed in a material world, man can forget the world of faith unless it is continually reinforced. Like human love, Christian faith needs to be experienced in concrete ways over and over again. Christ instituted the Eucharist precisely for this reason: Do this in memory of me.

Sunday Mass is intended to renew Christian faith on several levels at once. Like a prism, Sunday Mass draws to a focal point the diffuse and intangible world of faith, concretizing the centrality of God's saving action in every phase of human life. Because we are flesh and blood, we need the flesh and blood experience of Eucharistic liturgy to remain healthy Christians and to grow. If we do not have this weekly experience, the roots of our faith can quickly sicken and wither.

The parish Mass is a gathering of the local Christian community affirming the bonds uniting each person to the others. The congregation hears the word of God spoken and explained, and is invited to respond to God's word. By prayerfully entering into Christ's own sacrifice, we pledge ourselves once more to the great task of carrying forward the Father's plan for mankind's salvation. Nourished on the Body of the Lord, we are sent forth energized with fresh vision and strength.

Such is the ideal of Eucharistic Celebration. Every informed Catholic bears the responsibility to implement this ideal in his life as well as he can. This responsibility is implicitly incurred at Baptism, when one first accepts the gift of the Holy Spirit and commits himself to the cause of Christ.

But in practice one's responsibility toward the third commandment does not begin to function until this responsibility is consciously recognized and accepted. Presumably, the average adult Catholic is capable of accepting this responsibility. Too, Catholic parents must educate their children in this matter. A child needs help to grow to a point of personal maturity in faith, so that he can freely respond to the values inherent

in attending Sunday Mass regularly.

Providing this education is difficult, especially when dealing with teenagers. Growth in faith is marked by the same turbulent ups and downs, and the occasional moods of rebellion, that generally characterize adolescent growth. Parents and teachers must use great patience, knowing when to act and when not to. A young person whose baptismal commitment has not yet been consciously ratified, and who is struggling with growing pains of faith, is not always helped by being forced to attend Mass against his will. He is definitely

To trust in the law itself is to rest on the doorway without going in

not helped by being told that he commits a mortal sin by missing Mass.

To the former categories of mortal sin and venial sin, a third should be added: serious sin. Sin is not circumscribed by the exterior action. It is rooted in man's will. Between the poles of mortally sinful decisions and venially sinful decisions is a large gray area. For example, partners in marriage can offend each other in such a radical way that separation or divorce is the outcome. This is comparable to mortal sin in our relationship with God. On the other hand, a man and wife can hurt each other in little ways, which compares to venial sin. But between the two extremes there can be serious offenses — acts which seriously strain or threaten their relationship, yet do not dissolve it.

An informed Christian adult who misses Mass through laziness is seriously negligent toward the third commandment. But a child who skips Mass is not mature enough in his faith to be guilty of serious irresponsibility. Finally, a young adult who is turned off by his experience at parish liturgies and is sincerely trying to work through his personal faith problems, may not be guilty of serious sin by occasionally missing Mass. He could incur serious sin by not dealing with his faith problem. But until he straightens that out, his responsibility to ratify that faith by participating at Mass does not make too much sense. It goes without saying, of course, that experiencing good liturgies to confirm his faith may be what the person most needs.

Unfortunately, there are no easy answers. This much is clear. Faithful participation at Sunday Mass is the norm for every practicing Catholic. This is the law of the Church as well as the law of God. But the law is there for the good it fosters. To emphasize the law, rather than the good behind it, is to put the cart before the horse. Man was not made for the Sabbath; the Sabbath was made for man.

19

Is Confession Old-Fashioned?

In the late 1920s, the famous political figure Al Smith was waiting outside a confessional in a New York church. Recognizing him, the person at the head of the line motioned Smith to enter the confessional next. Smiling, Smith shook his head and whispered: "I'm in no more of a hurry to do this than anyone else."

Al Smith's attitude typified that of most Catholics a generation ago. No one especially enjoyed going to confession, but people were convinced that it had to be done, and fairly regularly. So most practicing Catholics made a point of receiving the sacrament of Penance once or twice a month.

A change is noticeable today. More often than not, there are no waiting lines outside the confessionals, not even on Saturday nights. Priests from different parishes and from different parts of the country notice the same thing. The number of confessions seems to be declining. Why is this so? Is it a sign of weakening faith?

Maybe it is, and maybe it is not. Undoubtedly, our age is experiencing some confusion in regard to confession. The ferment of renewal since Vatican II has touched every sector of Catholic life. Amid the turmoil of new ideas and changing practices, the easy certainties of pre-Vatican II days are frequently lacking. Going to confession never was very attractive, so the present confusion can provide, for some, an excuse to be less concerned about going to confession.

To lower one's esteem for the sacrament of Penance is a grave mistake. Ever since Christ gave His apostles power to forgive sin, the Church has always treasured this sacrament. On the other hand, not every generation in the past used Penance in the same way. At one period in early Church history, Penance was thought of as a once-in-a-lifetime sacrament. A person had recourse to it only if he reneged on his baptismal commitment in some flagrant and obvious way. Penance was then viewed as a second Baptism, reuniting him to Christ and to the Church as on the day of Baptism. It was tacitly agreed that such a rupture could not conceivably occur more than once in a man's lifetime, at least not with the hope of its being repaired.

We may regard this outlook of our forefathers as extreme. By the same token, they would doubtlessly have viewed as extreme the notion that man can fall into mortal sin quite regularly, and just as regularly go to confession. If they underplayed

Christian life is founded on the gospel, which is an invitation to freedom

human frailty, perhaps we overplay it.

Mortal sin is the sin which deals a mortal blow to man. By committing mortal sin, a person severs his basic orientation toward God and His salvation plan. This rupture happens knowingly and deliberately. As a result, man's entire life becomes radically redirected away from love and toward self-centerdness.

Moral theologians today generally agree that mortal sin takes place less frequently than we formerly supposed. Not enough allowance was made, in the past, for impedi-

ments to human freedom; and not enough gradation was made on moral scales between moral and venial sin. These conclusions stem from a better understanding of psychology, as well as from a more refined notion of the biblical meaning of sin.

Perhaps some people confess less often today because they are less likely to accuse themselves of mortal sin. In the past we were taught that the sacrament of Penance is necessary, strictly speaking, only in case of mortal sin. Therefore, people may conclude that they do not have to go to confession so often as they used to, if at all.

Again, strictly speaking, these people could be correct. The problem is, however, that they are making this decision in a legalistic context. The Christian life is not founded on technicalities of law, not even of sacred law. The Christian life is founded on the gospel, which is an invitation to freedom. We are heirs of Christ solely because we have been baptized into His death and resurrection. It is wrong to test the authenticity of our Christian commitment by the question: What does the law oblige us to do? The real question must be: How can we respond to God's overwhelming love, which we possess in the Person of the Holy Spirit?

The most important dimension of our daily experience is the underlying commitment made at Baptism to love God and to pursue His will. At any given moment, either we act to implement this "fundamental option," as moralists call it, or to impede it. Our Christian maturity can be measured in terms of how conscious we are of our all-inclusive commitment to the cause of Christ, and how earnest we are about living it out. "The fact is that whether you eat or drink — whatever you do — you should do all for the glory of God" (1 Corinthians 10:31).

From this perspective the sacrament of Penance takes on fuller, more accurate meaning. It is not a question of *having* to go to confession, but of *wanting* to go. Living out a marriage commitment has moments of tension and temporary estrangement. Humanly speaking, our commitment to our heavenly Father is no different. For a person to admit failures and to ask for forgiveness only when compelled to do so is adolescent at best.

We should go to confession not to be legally exonerated before God, but to trustfully ask His forgiveness and help. To the degree that a person is sensitive to God's love, he will be sensitive to his failure to return that love. The sacrament of Penance can etch these moments of insight and sorrow in deep and fruitful lines. To silently pray for God's mercy is good. To concretize our prayer by receiving the sacrament of Penance is better. We are less apt to forget our repentance, and are more conscious of the reality of God's mercy being extended to us. In addition, we are given a graphic reminder that sin is not just a private affair between us and God,

but that it involves responsibility to the whole of the Christian community, represented by the priest.

Ideally, then, we should receive the sacrament of Penance fairly frequently. Yet how often we do so is far less important than how meaningful our confession is. A brief and honest description of our overall relationship with God, concentrating on our weak points, is perhaps more effective than reciting a catalogue of sins.

In light of this discussion, we can see the reasonableness of postponing

> It is not a question of having to go to confession, but of wanting to go

a child's first confession beyond First Communion. Until a child is old enough to sense personal responsibility for his baptismal commitment to God, there is little to be gained by training him to confess irresponsible actions. When the experience of Christian repentance is as yet foreign to a child, premature confession creates the impression that the mechanics are what really count. When this happens, legalism begins to overshadow the true meaning of the gospel. Unfortunately, the impression can last a lifetime.

20

Have We Lost Our Sense of Prayer?

In contemporary Catholic life, one of the more confusing things is change in ways of praying. Older Catholics are distressed to see time-honored forms of prayer like novenas, benediction, and the rosary fading from use. The informal, sometimes talkative, style of today's Eucharistic Celebration contrasts sharply with past practice, when reverence and silence dominated. Religion teachers find today's students restless and disinterested when formal prayers are recited in class.

What is happening? Are we Catholics losing our taste for prayer? Or are we experiencing a healthy, though painful, transformation in the Church's prayer life?

In these restless times we must fall back on fundamentals. What is prayer? The old catechism definition will serve our purpose: Prayer is the lifting of our minds and hearts to God. In some sense every true prayer involves two things. First, there is a deliberate effort to lift one's consciousness above ordinary preoccupations. Second, there is communication with God in some way.

Prayer is at once our greatest privilege as Christians and our greatest responsibility. The mysterious Creator of the cosmos has revealed Himself to us in the person of His Son, Jesus Christ. Through Baptism we are placed in a state of permanent contact with God because His Holy Spirit dwells in us at all times. The goal of our lives is eternal union with God, when we will communicate with Him in full consciousness forever. Little wonder, then, that Saint Paul says: "never cease praying" (1 Thessalonians 5:17). Prayer is what life is really all about.

When we lift our consciousness to God, we are not making a gigantic mental leap to locate Him beyond the sky. God is with us at all times: ". . . he is not really far from any one of us. In him we live and move and have our being . . ." (Acts 17:27-28). Rather, we are lifting our attention from whatever prevents us from sensing God's immediacy.

God is not to be found on the borders of human experience; He is dead center. As one theologian puts it, God is the ground of being. Prayer, then, is an attempt to get in tune with the deepest core of all reality, including our own lives. Praying is like peeling an onion: we try to strip off, one by one, the outer layers of conscious attention to get at the center of it all.

We are immersed in God at all

> God is not to be found on the borders of human experience; He is dead center

times, like goldfish in water. We pray to get in harmony with the ground of our being. As young people might say, prayer is putting it all together. By affirming the central value of our life, we put ourselves in order. The countless interests and concerns of everyday existence are integrated in the discovery of God, the Master and the final goal of all.

The ideal of prayer is one thing, but to actually pray is something else. Prayer does not come easily, largely because we are so habituated to the lack of integration in our lives. We need help to overcome natural inertia. For this reason the Church has carefully treasured whatever insights have proved useful in the past. A study of Church history shows that forms of prayer have varied in keeping with forms of cultural milieu. What appeals to one generation may or may not appeal to the next, depending on whether the world view, or cultural frame of reference, changes or remains the same.

This is not to deny the permanence of some kinds of prayer. For instance, the Eucharist and the Lord's Prayer have always been primary in the Church's life. However, there have been surprising variations in practice. The Mass was celebrated quite differently in the early centuries of the Church. The Lord's Prayer is found in three places in the New Testament, but never in exactly the same words. The early Christians were far more concerned with the priorities set forth in Christ's prayer than with the wording.

The Fathers of Vatican II have asserted that ours is an age of major cultural change:

> Today, the human race is involved in a new stage of history. Profound and rapid changes are spreading by degrees around the whole world . . . Hence we can already speak of a true cultural and social transformation, one which has repercussions on man's religious life as well.
>
> (*Pastoral Constitution on the Church in the Modern World*, article 4)

Inevitably, in an age in which the world view is rapidly changing, persons will struggle to find new, more meaningful ways to pray. That is what the Church is experiencing today. There is conflict between inherited prayer forms — forms which many adult Catholics have come to cherish — and the new creative forms preferred by an impatient younger generation.

It is a mistake to make light of prayer forms that continue to nourish traditional Catholics. Those who downgrade the rosary forget that, for centuries, Catholics found in this simple prayer a mainstay of their lives. To dismiss novenas and benediction of the Blessed Sacrament because they are out of tune with contemporary theological horizons is not always justified. Education is not education when it is unnecessarily disruptive. Unless something updated and equally supporting can be found to replace these devotions, people may be left with a void in their prayer life.

On the other hand, adult Catholics should be responsibly sensitive to the fact that many traditional prayer forms no longer succeed with other people, especially the young. If the new style of liturgy tends to be less reverent for older people, it is also more meaningful for the younger. Set verbal formularies worked well in the past; spontaneous prayers work better today, as do songs and Bible readings. Past generations were conditioned to find God in private meditation, whereas the now genera-

tion finds God more readily in interpersonal communication.

God is present everywhere. That people search Him out in one way rather than another is nothing to be disturbed about. The fact impressed on us by Vatican II is that the present age, taken as a whole, tends to seek communication with God in ways unlike those of the past ages. The final outcome is not yet clear. There are many dangers in the interim. We can ignore the valuable experience of past ages.

> It is a mistake to make light of prayer forms that continue to nourish traditional Catholics

We can close ourselves off too quickly from radically fresh and more affective possibilities. We can throw up our hands in despair and cease to pray at all.

The challenge confronting us is to hold on to prayer, and to keep our balance between the old and the new. Parents and teachers have a uniquely difficult task in teaching the young to pray. We need a firm faith and an open mind. But most of all, we need to know authentic Christian prayer from personal experience. There is no substitute for doing the real thing.

21

The Priesthood and Religious Life: What Is Today's Challenge?

To serve God as a priest, brother or nun has always been considered an exceptional career. But this has never been so true as it is today. It is a fact that far fewer persons are entering seminaries, convents and novitiates now than was the case 10 years ago.

Although the number of recruits is dwindling, the demand for the services of professional religious is expanding. The shortage of priests is reaching crisis proportions. Statistics indicate that for every priest ordained in the United States last year, two men left the priesthood. The growing number of lay teachers needed in Catholic schools is one clear sign that sisters and brothers are faring no better.

What is behind the present shortage of vocations to the priestly and religious life? What can concerned teachers and parents do to foster vocations today?

In the first place, a large dose of realism is called for. If the entire Church is undergoing an unsettling experience in the wake of Vatican II, this is especially true for priests and religious. Church renewal and the modern theological movement have brought about change in traditional forms of religious life as much as they have renovated older liturgical forms, such as the Mass. Not all religious applaud these changes.

Not everyone understands or sympathizes with the new directions emerging for priestly and religious life. Not everyone who understands has the flexibility required to alter patterns of living thought to be irrevocable. Disagreement and discontent, never absent in some convents and in some rectories, tend

to be even more operative in the present age of transition.

The *esprit de corps* of priests and religious, taken as a whole, is no longer present as it was in pre-Vatican II days. Young people are quick to notice discontent, and seeing it causes them to think twice about getting personally involved. In addition, their exposure to post-Vatican II thinking makes young people aware of the enhanced role of the laity for the Church of the future. Why be a priest or sister if every baptized person is challenged to forward the priestly work of Christ? Besides, the Church today is turning outward more and more toward the world. A lay person is already at the center of the Church's concern; why go off to a convent or a seminary?

Another and more serious objection raised by young people is that religious life is irrelevant. By this charge they mean that the Church's work seems to have little relation to what is centrally important in the world's affairs. Everywhere dedicated people are immersed in problems of war, starvation, disease, injustice, overpopulation, and threats to the earth's environment. While present on the borders of these problems, the Church nevertheless seems primarily absorbed in preaching a religious message that nobody has time to hear.

The total picture appears to be pretty bleak. How is one to encourage vocations to religious life in view of these negative factors?

Certainly not by trying to whitewash the facts. Glossy brochures picturing ecstatically happy priests and nuns over a festive dinner are entirely out of place. Instead of romanticizing, we should speak the plain truth.

Christ never promised His chosen followers a life of ease. He spoke of hardship, suffering, and rejection. But He also spoke of a life of unparalleled value and meaning.

The purpose of the priesthood and of the religious life takes its definition from the purpose of the Church as a whole. As a segment of mankind, Christians have a crucial role to play. All men are called to unending peace, joy, and love. According to Vatican II, the Church is the sacrament of the unity of all mankind under God.

By consciously responding to the gospel, Christians sign forth God's saving action to the rest of the world. The Church is a leaven in the dough of world society, making the good news of Christ known and believable by translating it into loving service to mankind's deepest needs.

For one whose faith is alive, nothing is more relevant to the human race today and to its desperate problems than the Church. Every solution other than the gospel is incomplete or naive. Mankind cries out for a radical healing of the spirit far more than for a healing of material elements. Christ and the gospel do not simply offer a better solution; they constitute the world's only real hope.

However, the Church has not been doing its job very well, as young people frequently point out. Pope John XXIII did not dispute the point. He summoned a Council to awaken the Church and to reform it. No miraculous transformation has been noticeable yet. But it is under way. This is the bright side of these unnerving days after Vatican II. The Church is struggling to shake off its lethargy. Renewal is definitely in progress. If the cross is at hand, the resurrection will follow.

At the heart of renewal efforts, for better or for worse, are priests and religious. They are to Catholic lay people what the Church as a

> **The priests and the religious are living sacraments of Christ and the gospel**

whole is to the rest of mankind. The priests and the religious are living sacraments of Christ and the gospel. By lives of singular dedication, they make God's saving work tangible to others, so that they too can mobilize behind the cause of Christ. If the laity are not inflamed with Christ's vision for the world, then priests and religious do not sufficiently embody this vision in their lives.

The challenge to enter the priesthood or religious life today is magnified by the challenge given the entire Church by Vatican II. A revitalized laity is very much dependent upon a revitalized clergy. Without competent leadership from priests, sisters and brothers, the people of God as a whole will continue to give the world confused signals about the true meaning of Christ's redemption. If priests and religious become open to the power of the Holy Spirit, the entire Church will come alive — and then the entire world.

Admittedly, we are speaking of a dream. But it is the dream given us by Christ Himself. Furthermore, it is a dream which Christ guarantees will one day be realized. To be a Christian is to be committed heart and soul to the attainment of this dream. The obstacles to be overcome are immense. Causes for discouragement abound. Those who tend to look for security, who want maximum insurance for personal risks taken, are poor candidates for the priesthood or religious life today.

But for those who are truly committed to the gospel, who are looking for a singularly important way to benefit mankind, the priesthood and the religious life should hold top priority. The potential for action — real action — within the religious life is second to that within no other calling. The fields are indeed white for the harvest.

22

What Makes a Catholic a Catholic?

Time was when Catholics had not the least doubt about their identity. The Catholic Church was described in unmistakable terms as the one, true Church of Christ, outside of which there is no salvation. Further, it was claimed that the Catholic Church could be recognized for what it is. Christ gave His Church four identifying marks. His Church must be one, holy, catholic or universal, and apostolic. Only the Catholic Church possesses these marks.

What to make of people outside the Church was always a sticky question. It was unthinkable that non-Catholics were condemned wholesale to hell. The theory was that God judges each person according to his lights, and that sincere seekers of the truth can, therefore, be saved despite their ignorance of the true religion. It was further surmised that to whatever degree non-Catholics accept authentic elements of the gospel, they, thereby, become members of the Catholic Church in a hidden way. This supposition saved the principle that salvation comes only from the Catholic Church.

This line of thinking was framed largely within the historical context of the long, heated debate with Protestantism. Ever since the days of Martin Luther, Catholic theology has been torn between condemning Protestant religions as false, and upholding the possibility of salvation for Protestants.

The Second Vatican Council has not put the controversy entirely to rest, but it has dramatically changed the atmosphere of the different points of view. Hostility has given way to friendliness. Protestants are no longer referred to as heretics, but as separated brothers. The *Decree on Ecumenism* affirms that there is much good to be found in Protestantism. It invites Protestants not to enter the Catholic Church as such, but to join Catholics in a common search for a more authentic response to the gospel.

The last point is highly significant. The Catholic Church has renounced the assumption, sometimes implied in the past, that its response to Christ is perfect, or that the gospel is perfectly expressed in the Church's corporate life. Rather, the Catholic Church humbly professes itself to be a people in pursuit of the gospel and the will of Christ. Protestants take the same stance. United on this common ground, the ultimate reconciliation of all Christians becomes an eventual possibility.

The *Dogmatic Constitution on the Church* of Vatican II spells out in clear language that God's saving activity is not limited to the formal confines of the Catholic Church. Of Protestant Churches it is said:

> . . . we can say that in some real way they are joined with us in the Holy Spirit, for to them too He gives His gifts and graces whereby He is operative among them with His sanctifying power.

(article 15)

In successive statements, God's saving action is also affirmed to be operative among Jews, non-Christian religions, and even among those who ". . . have not yet arrived at an explicit knowledge of God . . ." (article 16).

In view of this official declaration that God is at work to save men of goodwill everywhere, we must ask what is unique about His activity in the Catholic Church. If we Catholics do not have a monopoly on Christ and on the Holy Spirit, what is special about us?

The question should be approached from two directions. First, what is special about being a Christian?

> Claims to uniqueness do not constitute a boast on the part of the Catholic Church, but a challenge

Second, what makes a Catholic a Catholic?

Granting the reality of Christian revelation, there is an obvious distinction between those who possess the gospel and those who do not. God has revealed Himself through Jesus Christ. To know Christ, and to be baptized into His life, is to guide one's destiny unerringly. Although the Holy Spirit works secretly in non-Christians, they are not aware of His action. To this extent they fumble through life blindly and without assurance.

Christians are able to be the eyes

and ears of mankind as a whole. A Christian knows what life is for. He knows the final goal of the evolving history of the human race. He can accurately identify and work to overcome the true obstacles to peace, justice, and happiness. In a word, Christians consciously possess the power to transform the world for the better, and to guide history toward its God-given destiny, the reconciliation of all things in Christ.

Together with other Christians, we Catholics share this awesome responsibility toward our non-Christian brothers. But how do we differ from non-Catholic Christians? This is the second part of our question.

In the first place, we stand by our perennial claim that we have inherited from the Church of the apostles all of the elements of authentic Christianity. We have not always lived up to the gospel as we should have. At times Protestants have shown greater sensitivity to certain aspects of the gospel than we have. But our basic assertion remains: The Catholic Church possesses the essentials of historical Christianity with a fullness lacking in other Churches. We alone have the complete liturgy, hierarchy, and teaching authority bequeathed to the apostolic Church by Christ.

A second aspect of our uniqueness is the historical service which the Catholic Church has rendered to Christianity as a whole. If all Christian denominations together form the one body of Christ, the Catholic Church has provided the bone structure for the whole. Historically, the Catholic Church has given Christianity stability and continuity. Through the doctrinal battles that have been waged in past centuries, the gospel has always been preserved and purified under the direction of the teaching office of the Catholic Church. What is counterfeit in Christian faith and practice has been carefully sifted from what is authentic.

Protestant communities have sometimes shown more creativity and flexibility in implementing one or another aspect of the gospel. But lacking the ballast of Catholic tradition and hierarchy. Protestants have also tended at times to lose sight of the gospel as a whole. The fine line of orthodoxy may become obscured for a time in the Catholic Church, but it is always there. And because it is always there, Christianity as a whole will always endure.

These claims to uniqueness do not constitute a boast on the part of the Catholic Church, but a challenge. "You will know them by their deeds" (Matthew 7:16). If we Catholics actually have greater access to the sanctifying resources of Christ than do Protestants, we must be more devoted to the gospel. We should be trying to prove not that other Christian Churches are wrong, but that we are totally immersed in the saving work of Christ. This kind of competition will be welcomed by our Protestant brothers. For then we will be working for the same objective, instead of arguing over who is better.

23

Should the Church Be Involved in Social Problems?

A recent meeting between seminary personnel and a group of lay people centered on what the average Catholic looks for in a parish priest. A point made with considerable emphasis was that Sunday sermons should steer clear of political and social issues. The old saying was cited: Politics and religion don't mix.

The saying comes from an age carefully taught to distinguish between the Church and the world, religion and life, body and soul, and the natural and the supernatural. The categories were kept separate both in theory and in practice. Religion looked to man's supernatural good; the Church's business was the immortal soul. Politics related to man's earthly existence only, and thus did not belong to the domain of religion.

Even on the grounds of pre-Vatican II theology, the model just described can be seriously challenged. Since the time of Leo XIII in the nineteenth century, many papal encyclicals have been addressed to political and social topics. The Church has never overlooked the corporal works of mercy, which apply the gospel directly to man's material needs. Schools, hospitals and orphanages have long testified to the Church's concern for man's social and bodily needs.

Still, in the past there was confusion about the extent of the Church's interest in the inner workings of social structures. In the Middle Ages things were different; the Church and the state were closely intertwined. But with the rise of nationalism, religion and politics learned to follow separate paths. The results of this are seen today in countries such as France and Mexico, where large Catholic majorities are governed by regimes guardedly indifferent to Church interests.

Until recently the Catholic Church in the United States was kept on the defensive in the political arena. Non-Catholics feared our intentions. It was thought that any concession to

Catholics by way of state-supported schools or election to public office could eventuate in an attempted Catholic take-over. Partly to ease this hostility, Catholics sometimes vauntingly proclaimed that religion has no place in politics.

After the Protestant Reformation, the self-image of the Catholic Church became narrowly defensive. The Church was viewed as a segment of society inwardly absorbed in its own good, apart from the rest of the world. The Church saw its mission

> **Vatican II has called a halt to this separatism between life and religion**

as concern for the welfare of its own members but not for the welfare of people outside the Church. The Church regarded itself as a fortress holding the enemy at bay, rather than as a leaven transforming the world.

Vatican II has called a halt to this separatism between life and religion. The *Dogmatic Constitution on the Church* dramatically reverses the concept of the Church as a self-serving organization, and declares that the Church is the visible instrument of Christ's saving love for man-

kind as a whole. The *Pastoral Constitution on the Church in the Modern World* details the fact that socio-political concerns are integrally tied in with concerns of the gospel and the Church.

Symbolic of a new era in Church history are the nuns who marched at Selma and Father Groppi, and the Berrigan brothers, no matter how we judge them. It is an era of direct involvement and personal participation on the part of the Church in the affairs of world society. Basically, there are two causes for this change in policy.

First, history of the Church's non-involvement has lowered its credibility in the eyes of needy people outside the Church. In genuine concern for the working classes, Karl Marx condemned the Church as an agent of capitalism, helping to keep social injustices from being righted. Philosophers such as Friedrich Nietzsche and Bertrand Russell, who championed the betterment of man, shared the conviction that the Church is an enemy of mankind's progress. As wrong as we find their judgments of the Church, they were intelligent spokesmen for large segments of the Western world.

The same criticism comes through in a more familiar way in the charge, often made by young people, that the Church is irrelevant to the most pressing problems of our age. Mankind as a whole is on the brink of revolution and despair because of the enormity of its common problems: war, poverty, racism, and exploitation in many forms. It is this human race, with all its frustrations and fears, that is the object of God's love today and of the good news of His Son's dawning reign over the world. Yet all too often the Church's voice has been muffled. People say they cannot believe because they have so little evidence that the Church really cares for them.

The second cause for the present intensification of social and political action by the Church is a renewed understanding of its mission. In the

> ## We have the responsibility to do all we can to right social wrongs

timeless words of Saint Paul, the Church is "the body of Christ" (1 Corinthians 12:27). The body is the material, visible element of an unseen life-force called the soul. Christ Himself is not visible in the world today. But He is very much alive. His life-force is the Holy Spirit, who is at work in men of goodwill everywhere to renew the face of the earth.

The Church is the visible organization which signs forth Christ's presence and the power of the Holy Spirit for all the world to see. Jesus can be identified today by the same works

that made Him known in gospel times. He went out to the poor and to the oppressed. He healed; He comforted; "He went about doing good . . ." (Acts 10:38). United by Baptism, we Christians are commissioned to carry on this very work, and thus make Christ known in the world today. We have the responsibility to do all we can to right social wrongs, and to utilize whatever political means are available to us to do this.

There is danger, of course, of going to an extreme. In the final analysis, Christ is not a glorified social worker. He brings a more lasting healing to human ills. He gives His life to fulfill and immortalize our own. Ultimately, Christ stands more for the eradication of sin than for the eradication of breadlines. But for too long, the clergy have gone to the opposite extreme by preaching a gospel devoid of practical social consciousness. This is not the gospel recorded by Saints Matthew, Mark, Luke and John.

Since Vatican II the Church has been asking us to remember that Christ stands in our midst as one who serves. That means we are His servants to the rest of the world. Christ's own words tell us that our worth to Him will finally be measured, not by what we have done to save ourselves, but by what we have done to save others:

> For I was hungry and you gave me food, I was thirsty and you gave me drink. I was a stranger and you welcomed me. . . .
> (Matthew 25:35)

24

Where Will It All End?

The mood of mankind today is increasingly reflective. It is as if we had become exhausted from the breathless pace of progress, and had decided to pause and think. As Alvin Toffler puts it in his best seller, modern man suffers from "future shock." For other generations change came more slowly and was digested more easily. Our generation is the first in history to confront continuous change as the normal pattern of life.

Another way to say it is that our ancestors were too busy staying alive to be very philosophical about life itself. Food had to be obtained. Clothes had to be made and mended. Money had to be scraped together to pay bills for the necessities. People were too immersed in keeping life going to ask what it all meant or how it all fit together.

Today's typical college student symbolizes the new generation. He worries more about the meaning of life and of society than about the expenses of a college education. If his family cannot finance his education, he can get a government loan. Even if he is low on cash, he does not fret over getting food; there are too many available possibilities. Relatively free of material concerns, he has the enviable luxury to ponder life's ultimate question: What is it really all about?

Hurtling together through the trackless expanses of cosmic space, mankind today is turning its attention from the logistics involved in being fellow passengers to the ques-

tion of the journey itself. Where are we going? What is the direction of future history? To what extent can we control our common destiny? Where will it all end?

Many answers are offered to these questions. Depending upon which theory is followed, mankind divides into different camps. Some take a pessimistic position. They point out that our planet has reached the halfway point in its ability to sustain human life. Unless we destroy ourselves first, in five billion years man's history will culminate in the oblitera-

We who have faith share responsibility to improve the Church and make the gospel credible

tion of man together with his spaceship earth. Ultimately, according to this theory, life is meaningless.

Other people follow theories that transcend the physical level. They point to the fact that man's greatest asset is his power to reason. Man experiences an immaterial world by means of thought. He loves. He feels loneliness. He knows courage. He is enthralled by beauty. He honors truth. But do these ethereal experiences have objective meaning? Is the desire for goodness, truth and beauty evidence that they are real?

The religions of the world are one in answering this question in the affirmative. Christianity, like Buddhism and Muhammadanism, insists that life has a value transcending the level of sense perception. All religions agree that man's instinctive struggle to pursue good and to avoid evil underscores the final meaning of life. They also agree that love, in its authentic form, lies at the heart of the human quest.

Among the religions of the world, what is unique about Christianity? First, its historical credentials are without rival. Some 2000 years ago, a man named Jesus was known to have lived and died in an obscure corner of the Roman Empire. His followers claimed that He rose to new life, and that He had become God's permanent agent for the renovation and final perfection of the human race.

The claim was not well received. Persecution broke out, first among the countrymen of Jesus, then wherever Christians could be found in the whole of the Roman Empire. Yet nothing could halt the spread of Christianity. It outlived its persecutors and eventually took hold in every corner of the world.

Equally important, the internal credentials of Christianity are without parallel. Tested by millions of people in the course of time, the vision of life known as the gospel continues to win credence from scholars as well as from the uneducated. This vision gives meaning and totality to life because it resonates with every facet of human experience, integrating the parts within a comprehensive whole. For the gospel testifies to God's saving action in man's history; its testimony is found to be true by the test of man's own experience.

The good news of Jesus Christ explains that the cosmos is created and sustained by an omnipotent and all-good Being, who is God the Father. God has made man in His own image, inviting all men to enter into His own everlasting life. Evil can be identified both as man's present state of incompletion, which causes him to yearn for what is yet to come, and as sin, which is man's failure to cooperate with God in completing creation.

God sent His Son to overcome evil. Risen and forever alive in power, Jesus now imparts His Holy Spirit to men of goodwill everywhere. All history progresses toward the day of Christ's visible return at the end of time, when creation will be complete and the happiness of redeemed mankind will be assured.

Evidence for the activity of the Holy Spirit is especially found in the Church. The Church on earth is a society of sinners. It is not, itself, the goal of creation; rather, it is the sign and the special instrument of God's saving action in men everywhere. Because Christians themselves are not immune from evil, they do not constitute a clear and unambiguous sign of God's love in the world. Imperfections in the Church will always provide justification for some people's disbelief.

We who have faith, however, share responsibility to improve the Church, and thus make the gospel credible. By virtue of Baptism, we have committed ourselves to make the gospel known, to embody the gospel in a community of living faith, and to witness the gospel through generous service to the needs of all men. For these are the overarching purposes of the Church; to be a Christian is to do these things as best we possibly can.

Never before has mankind so much needed the light of the gospel. Never before in history has the human community been so attuned to the question of life's ultimate meaning, or so desperately in search of the answer. Never before, therefore, have Catholics faced such a singular challenge. The Second Vatican Council has called for the renewal of the Church in the light of this challenge. By responding, we can change the face of the earth. We can open mankind to its future. And there is no doubt about it: it is a future worth working for, because the news we bring is good news!

Never before
has mankind so much
needed the light of
the gospel

"From Confusion to Confidence"– What Is It?

Just how much confidence do you have in yourself as a religion teacher? Confidence in the message? Confidence built with other teachers? Confidence in your students?

After three or four religion classes, does your enthusiasm wane a bit? Can you use help in motivating your students?

Can you use educational games effectively? Games students can and will play? Creative techniques for classroom success? Can you use films and other audio-visuals effectively in class?

FROM CONFUSION TO CONFIDENCE will prove a valuable help to you with these and other problems in your religion class. Published less than a year ago, this book has 24 easy-to-read chapters, written by professional religious educators and experts in related fields.

FROM CONFUSION TO CONFIDENCE, because it zeroes in on 24 of the biggest problems the religion teacher faces, has been widely used in teacher training courses throughout the United States and Canada. The price — only $1.25.

Also published by HI-TIME Publishers, Inc.:

HI-TIME — the weekly religion text for high school students

Better Teaching — the teacher edition which accompanies each issue of HI-TIME

Focus on HOPE — a series of seven issues published twice a year: in the spring and in the fall. Designed for adult study and discussion in the parish and for informative reading in the home. Five series are now available.

For information on any of the materials and books published by HI-TIME Publishers, Inc., please write:

HI-TIME Publishers, Inc.
Box 7337
Milwaukee, WI 53213